MW00941038

What's My Next Move

By Richard LeBrun

Research: Viel Elysse Cancsino

Cover Design by Andrea Viernes,

Virtually Done For You Digital Marketing

ISBN-13: 978-1727138856

ISBN-10: 1727138856

WHAT'S MY NEXT MOVE?

THE JOURNEY BACK TO SUCCESS FOR EXECUTIVES IN TRANSITION

Aknowledgements

I felt compelled to write this book to document the journey I found myself going on as an executive who found himself in a career transition and was encouraged by my wife, Cathy, to share this with my fellow colleagues. I want to thank my wife for her patience and support as I took on this new challenge. Never having written a book before, I knew this was going to be a task I could not do alone. Cathy has been my partner for 43 years. I could not see going this alone.

As part of my team, I want to personally thank my assistant, Viel Cansino, for her research and willingness to go the extra mile to find those golden nuggets of information. Furthermore, I want to share my deep appreciation for my Marketing Director, Andrea Viernes, for her creativity, intelligence and support and who has stood by me as we developed the idea and began to layout the plan to pull together all the needed pieces to make this a success.

I also want to thank all my colleagues that I have had the pleasure to meet and interview who have gone through a career transition, as well as those who were professional recruiters who were willing to offer their expert advice on the current condition of the job market, specifically for executives who are between the ages of 45 & 65. It was very important that I was able to capture the truth of what the market place is saying in order to best advise my readers how to navigate their transition successfully.

Lastly, I want to thank my friends and family who kept challenging me and offering encouragement to complete the book and that saw this as being important not just to me but for others who may need help in their career journey.

The market is changing at a very rapid pace and there appears to a frantic mindset held by Corporate America to mold and shape their organization in order to keep in step. I haven't found anyone with the answer to all our questions as it relates to how politics, international trade, robotics, artificial intelligence and the loss of industry knowledge from the retiring baby boomers will affect jobs going forward but what I have found is that, for older executives, the journey has been more difficult than they or I had anticipated.

The best advice I can offer at this time is for executives to be more strategic in their approach to their career transition and encourage them to look at all available possibilities in order to help themselves determine what their next move is going to be. I hope this book will serve you well in that endeavor.

Contents

Introduction

Thank you for taking time to read my book. It is my hope that this book can capture the journey that I and hundreds of others like me, in middle to upper senior level positions in their career between the ages of 45-65, will go through late in their career or find themselves stuck in a job that has stolen their quality of life and now are asking themselves, **What's My Next Move** ?

The book will describe how our human desire to improve the quality of life has led to what is now called *"Technological Unemployment"* and give reason for the change in the employment market due to economic and technological changes and understand that they had no control over what was to come. It will describe the new business model set in place for decades forward. The book will capture the emotional and practical side of what my colleagues from around the world have expressed to me.

I will have you look at the five options that each one of us face and must navigate with regard to our careers.

1- Retirement

2- Work for Corporate America

3- Start up a new company

4- Buy an existing company

5- Buy a franchise

Lastly, I offer a comparison of business ventures that will provide food for thought and serve as a beginning on the road map to venture out from the old norm called *"Corporate America"* to controlling your destiny through business ownership.

It is my hope that when you've finished reading you will be better equipped to take the next step to determine what your NEXT MOVE will be for you and your family.

Chapter 1

My Story

My name is Rich and I am currently 64 years old and a successful franchise consultant. Three years ago, I was 61with a successful career in commercial real estate for over 30 years. I began my career in 1982, working in downtown Chicago at the height of the 1980's recession when interest rates were 19%. Prior to this time, I worked in Lake Tahoe, Nevada where I was responsible for building condominiums for local investors. I had a successful career and worked for some of the largest companies in Chicago, where I was responsible for the real estate holdings of some of the largest pension funds, insurance companies and corporations in the country. I was fortunate enough to be part of companies that had the drive to be number one in the industry and became known as award-winning among their peers.

During my career, I was only out of work a maximum of eight months due to corporate selloff. I was in my 40's at the time, however, I was easily able to weather the storm. As I climbed the ladder, I held senior-level executive positions. Heading into my late 50's, everything was on track to finish my career at the peak of my performance.

As life would have it, the unexpected happened. I was managing our company's largest client who decided to exit the real estate market and sell off their entire multi-hundred-million-dollar portfolio. This caused a major financial shift and a restructuring within the company I was working for and thereafter I found myself in the job market. As a senior executive for the largest real estate company in Chicago, I thought surely, I would find another position easily. To the contrary, it became a much more difficult and frustrating journey than I ever anticipated. What I came to realize was there were a minimal number of executive level positions in the marketplace that required my skill set and the people holding these positions were not about to give them up.

I went down the traditional path of contacting friends, family and fellow colleagues. It was an endless cycle of rewriting resumes, working on social media and networking on a continual basis. The industry had changed a lot when it came to finding work. You no longer talk with anybody, but simply submit your resume online to the cold dark abyss called the internet and pray you receive a call.

During my interviews, I found that although my experience was welcome, there was this subtle way of letting me know they were looking for someone who was younger with growth potential. The companies were much more concerned about where I was in my stage of life and how that would play out for their future. I can't exactly blame them for having these thoughts. I remember doing the same thing when I oversaw the hiring process. I found myself negotiating against myself by suggesting that the employer pay me substantially less than what I was asking. In exchange, they will get someone with much higher level of experience. Although this sounded good from my perspective, the employers didn't appear to be interested.

Do this long enough and one begins to ask themselves, "Am I done?" I'm 61 years old and I worked my entire career, but no one is interested in capitalizing on my years of experience. I began to start evaluating where I was in relationship to retirement and quickly found out that I've yet to hit the mark I set out for myself. That would take at least another 7-10 years to reach. This created an emptiness inside me. Doubt started settling in and I found myself asking "Am I really finished with my purpose to add value to anyone?" and "How can I go from a leader to obscurity so quickly? More often than I care to admit, my faith had been challenged. My emotions as well my physical, financial, and social well-being were put on the table to be scrutinized.

Then, it happened. I attended a family event and began talking with my brother-in-law about business in general. He was an attorney. He mentioned he was about to close on buying a franchise. I proceeded to ask him "Why would you leave the legal profession to buy a franchise?" He explained how he was looking for recurring income, something that he could build to leave to his kids and was tired of the legal industry.

I went home that night and gave this quite a bit of thought. I began searching the internet for the word "franchise" and started reviewing the many brands that came up. I went down the path of investigating and began to learn the intricacies of purchasing a couple different franchise opportunities. To my surprise a whole new world of opportunity just opened up.

On my journey, I came across a franchise consultant who acted as my coach. He asked the right questions which took me down the path to help zero in on the type of franchise that would meet my goals, objectives and leadership style. I eventually asked him to describe in more detail what he did and why. He explained he was a franchise consultant and he did this because he wanted to help other people like himself who were executives in transition. This was 100% commission position and yet he wished he could've done it 10 years ago because it met all the needs that he was seeking to fill. Three years later, here I am, successfully operating as a franchise consultant with the country's leading firm. I was never in sales at any time in my career and never thought I would be good in this position. I originally bought a franchise to learn the industry and then ventured into my current company. I find the franchise industry to be extremely exciting and dynamic. The franchise model is what is called America's best-kept secret.

We, as consumers, purchase products or services from franchises on a daily basis throughout this country, but most don't understand how the business model works. The franchise industry is looking for those executives who understand business and what it takes to grow a company. This aligns perfectly to those who are now my clients. My clients are typically executives between the ages of 45 and 65 who find themselves in a career transition. Most are out of work, but many are frustrated with going through their third or fourth merger. These executives are living under the same gray cloud of uncertainty about the longevity of their careers that plagued me previously. They also have found their workload has increased exponentially to the detriment of their quality of life. They too have looked at the timeline of retiring and found they are 10 to 15 years short of reaching that goal and are now asking the same question I once asked, "What's My Next Move?"

I feel strongly about helping my fellow colleagues who were in the same situation as I was, letting them know about the franchise model. I firmly believe that of all the options, the franchise model will meet my clients' goals and objectives the best. My clients are risk averse, they want speed to market and to capitalize on the expertise they have built throughout their career. There is no better model for business model than the franchise model to achieve this.

In franchising there is a saying "You are in business for yourself but not by yourself". When you are fearful and need to make an investment in yourself using some of your money that you earmarked for retirement, this becomes a major decision worth spending the right amount of time evaluating your options. You do not want to do this on your own. You want a team of proven, successful individuals who will deliver and help you succeed, which the franchise model offers.

If you were to call me today, I would tell you I wish I would've made the move 10 years ago. If you would have asked me 10 years ago, "did I ever see myself in sales?", the answer would have been "absolutely not". However, today I get to work from home, my business is portable, so I can work anywhere in the world I chose. I make a very good income and get to work with people all over the country, helping them achieve their goals in life by giving them hope for their future and showing them how to break through that barrier of concern about retirement.

I could ask for nothing more rewarding!

Allow me to take you on the journey that I went on. In the end I admit owning your own business is not for everyone, but I feel strongly to be able to make that determination for yourself it is important to be willing to take the time to explore the possibilities. You owe it to yourself and your family. Trust yourself and let the facts lead you to the right decision.

Chapter 2

The New Business Model

Tell me the truth. Would you rather pay $20 for a hamburger or $5.00? $2,000 for a TV or $300? Of course, as a consumer we all want to pay the lowest price possible, yet we don't realize that we as individuals put pressure on the economy to be competitive at all costs even if it leads to job loss. Companies are constantly managing their margins, finding ways to hold prices down, gaining market share, increasing their quality of product and service as well as marketing their brand. A company's profitability is always made up of labor and materials, (whether they are bought domestically or globally) and their ability to manage these costs. However, labor is the costliest line item in producing a product or service.

With regards to labor, to stay competitive in the world's economy, corporations are forced to make a choice; replace labor with technology or outsource to another country where labor rates are lower. As consumers, our choices drive unemployment. We say we want to support a $15 an hour minimum wage, which is great but, yet we are unwilling to spend $20 for that hamburger. This being the case, the owner must find ways to produce the product at a price we are willing to pay.

Bring on technology and robotics.

Today jobs that can be considered random or routine will be replaced by robots. You say this will affect only a certain segment of the market not for senior executives, right? Here is where the trickle up effect takes place. Prior to robotics, let's say an executive who managed a store or division would oversee a staff of 30 efficiently which would equate to one manager per store. Let's assume robotics can reduce staff down to 10 workers. That means the manager can now manage three stores with the same level of efficiency. For the employer who once had 9 stores with 9 managers and 270 employees, they now have 9 stores but only 3 managers and 90 employees. The important thing to note is the jobs that were lost are not coming back. They are permanently gone.

Management positions eventually eliminate a regional position and ultimately a potential higher-level job. Now, instead of five layers of management between the CEO and the line worker, only two are needed. Three prior positions are now gone, not to return. The term that is used is "Flat Organizational Structure".

I believe the consumer plays a role in the future of our economy and workforce. Yet, I also believe we are called to be good stewards of our resources. For the near future, the five-dollar hamburger will always win in the end.

Let's look how this all began.

Chapter 3

The Economy

The United States of America is the leading nation in basic and applied research for innovations that improve economic performance, according to the latest International World Competitiveness Yearbook. America is the front-runner in economic competitiveness. America excels in higher education and training. In fact, the country has become the number one choice destination for science and engineering graduate students and post doctorate scholars who wish to study abroad since World War II. Therefore, it comes as no o surprise that America—which comprises 6% of the world's population—produces more than 20% of the world's doctorates in science and engineering.

But what do these figures mean?

With such high regard for research and the vast numbers of scientists, engineers and other fields in this country, there are more and more advanced technologies and robotics being made to improve the quality of life. A market research firm, Gartner, predicts that companies not only in America but worldwide would spend 3.5 trillion on I.T. alone over the next few years. These rising tech trends are becoming mainstream. The question is "What would this mean for the economy and its workforce"?

There are so many tech trends on the rise such as artificial Intelligence (AI), advanced machine learning, virtual assistants, virtual and augmented reality and digital twins, to name a few. Artificial Intelligence or AI has become popular these days. While it used to be a far-off dream in the minds of sci-fi writers, it has now become reality. In fact, Google and Microsoft led this movement by adding AI to their services. These newly developed AI systems can understand, learn, predict, adapt and even, operate autonomously. The AI market is predicted to grow from $420 million in 2014 to $5.05 billion in 2020.

According to Grand View Research, the global Intelligent Virtual Assistant market size is expected to reach $12.28 billion by 2024. Why wouldn't it with such potential? While Siri, Cortana and Google Now had already been introduced to us, developers had found a way to refine them further to include more services. One fine example of this is Siri. When Apple finally opened Siri to third party developers, Siri was upgraded and had a new function of sending a payment to someone via Venmo when instructed. Have you brought Amazon's "Alexa" into your home?

The same goes for AR/VR technology. AR/VR technology can be both used for entertainment and work. In 2017, Microsoft will be releasing a new *HoloLens* which is made specifically for work. Facebook has even previewed work applications in Oculus Rift. IDC predicts that worldwide revenues for the augmented reality and virtual reality (AR/VR) market will grow from $5.2 billion in 2016 to more than $162 billion in 2020.

The technology that affects the economy and human labor the most is industrial robots. An industrial robot is defined as "an automatically controlled, reprogrammable, and multipurpose [machine]." These are the machines that do not necessarily require humans for them to operate and could perform multiple manual tasks. Research shows that for every additional robot, US economy reduces employment by 5.6 workers. Furthermore, every robot that is added to the workforce per 1,000 human workers causes wages to drop by as much as 0.25-0.50%.

Experts predict that the inventory of robots in the US will quadruple by 2025, jumping to 5.25 more robots per thousand workers (there are currently about 1.75 industrial robots in the US per 1,000 workers). This will serve to reduce the employment-to-population ratio by 0.94 to 1.76 percentage points, while resulting in 1.3 to 2.6% lower wage growth between 2015 and 2025. The addition of 5.25 more robots per thousand workers could also amount to a staggering 1.9 to 3.4 million additional job losses in just a decade. All of this is assuming the economies of the future behave the same way as the economy does today in response to additional automatons in the workforce.

Considering the imports from China and Mexico, outsourcing work to a global economy, the decline of routine jobs with industrial robots and other tech trends such as AI, these are the factors that without a doubt contribute to "technological unemployment".

MIT's Daron Acemoglu and Boston University's Pascual Restrepo found in their research that because there are relatively few robots in the US economy, the number of jobs lost due to robots has been limited so far (ranging between 360,000 and 670,000 jobs). However, they pose that if the spread of robots proceeds as expected by experts over the next two decades, the effects of having more and more robotics introduced into the workforce will be much more substantial.

Having a vast number of robotics at the country's disposal and with the rise of artificial intelligence, no job is totally, one hundred, percent safe. In addition to the routine labor force, one of the sectors that can be greatly hit with technological unemployment is middle/upper management.

In both good and bad economies, a knee jerk reaction for companies is to lay off employees to increase profits. The companies would then proceed to invest more on robotics to accomplish more work at a lesser labor cost. The main cutback would therefore fall on the middle/upper management. Managers, both leaders and subordinates, are paid more but they aren't exactly at the top of the corporate food chain nor are they the essential subordinates. With these recessions, some companies might find it necessary to let go of people and invest more in technology since they can be more efficient and cheaper in the long run.

Chapter 4

Job Duration

According to the U.S. Bureau of Labor Statistics, the median number of years that wage and salary workers had been with their current employer was 4.2 years in January 2016, down from 4.6 years in January 2014. It is important to note that older works (55+) had an average 10-year tenure while in the workforce and therefore have skewed the numbers. The number when removing the workers 55+ from the total brings the average tenure to just under three years.

Among the major occupations, workers in management, professional, and related occupations had the highest median tenure (5.1 years) in January 2016. Within this group, employees with jobs in management occupations (6.3 years), architecture and engineering occupations (5.5 years), and legal occupations (5.5 years) had the longest tenure. Workers in service occupations, who are generally younger than persons employed in management, professional, and related occupations, had the lowest median tenure (2.9 years). Among employees working in service occupations, food service workers had the lowest median tenure, at 1.9 years.

Now through in-depth research with recruiters around the country is has now been confirmed that the average length of a job for those between the ages of 45 to 65 and in a position of middle management or higher, is **less than two years**.

The definition of an older worker is getting younger. It appears to be going down in five-yearly increments. Forget 65 think 50 or even 45 today. Let's face the cold, hard truth. With the devastating downturn the economy experienced in 2008, middle/upper level managers in their 40s to 60s had become the vulnerable group for getting laid off. They are facing a downsized job market which, scholars and economists alike agree, is going to stay that way for a long time. These managers are much more expensive than their younger counterparts. Add that to the huge development of information technology that makes work easier and faster, further reducing the need for multiple levels of management.

While U.S. recessions since the oil crisis in the early 1970s each had their special causes and victims, the recent recession appears to be far deeper and longer than any of its predecessors. What does this mean for our middle/upper managers?

What companies must do to keep up with this economy is to restructure the organization, scrapping the more traditional "top down" or "bottom up" structure. A big number of modern companies opt to be flatter and downsized to be more flexible, competitive and innovative. This new flat and leaner structure reduces middle levels of management seeing it as unnecessary and outdated fat. This perspective is even further reinforced by technology. With companies investing in technology, these managers may find themselves lacking some of the high-tech savviness needed to succeed in a more efficient workplace companies are gearing towards.

While white collar management skills will always be in demand in some industries, middle-aged employees across the board will have a harder time positioning themselves relative to younger workers who have these set of new skills. This is especially true considering that over the past decade, the pace of technological change has picked up and the benefits of knowing the new technologies have increased. It's the younger workers who will be in a better position to take advantage of new job opportunities.

"Many companies, perhaps more so in this recession than in earlier ones, targeted mid-level managers for cuts," says Cornell's Freedman, partly because the service sector "saw dramatic expansion in the ranks of middle-level managers over the past two decades, which means they are a natural target" for cost-cutting.

In May 54.9% of job seekers over 55 had been scouting jobs for 27 weeks or more. According to the AARP Public Policy Institute, unemployed people over 55 have been out of work for more than a year or for 56 weeks on average.

The Urban Institute released a report showing that median monthly earnings fell 23% after an unemployment spell for reemployed workers aged 50 to 61, compared with just 11% for workers aged 25 to 34.

Under the Age Discrimination in Employment Act of 1967, age discrimination is illegal. The law prohibits treating job applicants or employees who are over age 40 less favorably because of their age. But most of the complaints filed with the U.S. Equal Employment Opportunity Commission focus on age-biased terminations rather than hiring discriminations. This is simply because hiring discrimination is so difficult to prove.

A recent study by economists at the University of California at Irvine and Tulane University found strong evidence of age discrimination in hiring, particularly for older women. The researchers sent out 40,000 dummy job applications that included signals on the job-seekers' ages and then monitored the response rates. They measured callback rates for various occupations; workers age 49-51 applying for administrative positions had a callback rate 29% lower than younger workers and it was 47% lower for workers over age 64. Indeed in July reported 29% of older full-time workers age 55-64 were in bad jobs. They were earning less than two-thirds of the median wage for workers in that age range.

When older displaced workers do find new jobs, they typically go back to work with about 60-75% of their former pay. These income disruptions play havoc with retirement plans. Nearly half of current retirees retire earlier than planned, according to survey research by the Employee Benefit Research Institute and 60% of older workers who experience job loss end up retiring involuntarily, according to the Center for Retirement Research at Boston College. Lost income in the decade leading to retirement can cut into future Social Security earnings by reducing the credits used to calculate a worker's benefits. It also can force workers to file for benefits early, sharply reducing lifetime benefits.

This segment of the labor market has turned to what is called "Piece Meal" approach to managing their careers until they reach retirement. You will find many of them have turned to multiple jobs in consulting, teaching, the trades or retail to balance out their income needs.

Today, there has been an increased interest in business ownership to secure their income. Most remember well the recession of 2008 and since then multiple mergers and acquisitions and are now looking forward into the future, dusting off the entrepreneurial spirit and investigating owning a business as a side job to build a platform to step off onto should they become the next corporate casualty.

Chapter 5

Entrepreneurship

If courage would have a profession, it would probably be an entrepreneur. Entrepreneurship means embarking on the risk of new enterprise. The word itself, "entrepreneur" comes from a French word which literally translates to "undertaker." Entrepreneurship, in its very essence, means managing the unknown and risking comfort zones for the potential of great rewards.

The very fabric of America is stitched and woven by entrepreneurs. The great American dream is pursued by many entrepreneurs which, in turn, lead the country to great economic growth which set our economy apart from other nations. A wise man by the name of Alex de Tocqueville once said, "The Americans always display a free, original, and inventive power of mind." These are the traits that can best describe a good entrepreneur, (but more on that later).

Now how did America come to be the land of entrepreneurs and how true is it until now? To answer that, let's have a quick run-down of American history and look at how this nation was founded by none other than, entrepreneurs.

Entrepreneurship existed way back in ancient times. Traders and merchants were the world's first entrepreneurs. The locals used a barter system where goods were being exchanged for another. They used to trade obsidian which is a black volcanic glass used for arrow heads with other much needed goods. Soon after that, people learned to domesticate animals and began to dabble in agriculture. When methods of agriculture had improved and became more sophisticated, people were able to build permanent homes and settle into an area because of the dependable food source. Cities and towns began to flourish. Nomads became less and less. People began to settle down and sought ways to improve their communities even more.

Time passed, settlements grew bigger and bigger and institutions were built. These institutions provided a new set of needs that further developed specialized roles for people by creating jobs in pottery, tool making, masonry, carpeting and many others.

Development didn't just stop there. People were starting to realize how they can make their living conditions so much better. Soon trade routes between the cities were made. Animals such as donkeys, horses and camels were used in transporting not only goods but also ideas and cultures as well as from one human settlement to another. With the exchange of goods and sharing of cultures, even more complex structures were built such as the Great Pyramids in Cairo and the temples in Sumeria. When the trade routes opened, this enabled people from different cultures to interact and form thousands of other subcultures.

Trade routes soon expanded, and everything was suddenly possible! Salt from Africa reached Rome, rice traveled from China to Asia, and the secrets of making paper were transferred from China to Europe. Arab traders brought coffee, lemons, and oranges to Europe for the first time. Of course, while trade is quicker and more efficient today, imagine how huge a leap this was to mankind thousands of years ago.

Early trade mainly focused on the barter system where item A was exchanged for item B, allowing one glaring flaw in that system. Both parties must have equal desire for what each party had. It doesn't take much to know that that does not happen fairly that often. Therefore, the clamor for trade made way for the money system. Before 2000 BC silver rings or bars were thought to have been used as money in ancient Iraq. Early forms of money (called specie) also included commodities like seashells, tobacco leaves, large round rocks, or beads.

When population started booming around 1470, trade grew even more and boom! Market was created. Capitalism had begun. Our early entrepreneurs, most often merchants and explorers, began to raise capital, take risks, and stimulate economic growth. But would you believe that early in the history of capitalism, the idea of monetary gain was looked down on by the members of high society? The practice of usury, charging interest on loans, was banned by the Christian Church. Jobs were assigned by tradition and caste. Innovation was stifled, and efficiency was forcefully put down, sometimes punishable by death.

Which brings us to America or the "New World".

In the classic "Free to Choose", Milton Friedman wrote, "Ever since the first settlement of Europeans in the New World, America has been a magnet for people seeking adventure, fleeing from tyranny, or simply trying to make a better life for themselves and their children." It began with Christopher Columbus and the Mayflower. In seeking new trade routes for tea and spices, the group stumbled upon America. It became the home for these colonial settlers. The stark quality all entrepreneurs have in common is their ability to take risks. These early settlers were the exact embodiment of entrepreneurs. They could shed their old lives, leave everything behind to seek greater prospects for themselves in the New World—into the vast unknown. In 1607, the Virginia Company sent three ships across the Atlantic Ocean. The 109 surviving passengers were unloaded at what became Jamestown, Virginia in the hopes of creating better lives for themselves.

Currently, research shows that unemployed jobseekers have a higher probability of owning their own businesses than fully employed workers. This implies that underemployed workers may just be the most entrepreneurial of us all. With the great economy we are experiencing today, companies are still downsizing left and right with middle managers taking the full brunt of it all. Downsizing can in fact breed entrepreneurship among the affected employees, especially older executives. Apparently, the process of job destruction can plant seeds of creativity! Downsizing (defined as a reduction in the number of man-years of at least 25 percent during the base-year) clearly encourages entrepreneurship. Working in a downsizing firm implies roughly a doubling of the probability of becoming an entrepreneur. Again, as a large fraction of employees are forced to leave, some will go for entrepreneurship. It is particularly interesting that the process of creative destruction apparently is two-sided: Not only does creativity cause destruction, as new and innovative firms push antiquated firms out of the market; destruction also causes creativity, as redundant workers and workers at risk of redundancy seek new ways to support themselves.

Even in a good economy, there is even more motivation to encourage new, entrepreneurial firms. When people and firms are not making money, it is necessary to make ends meet with unconventional and radical ways such as entrepreneurship.

How can entrepreneurship prove to be beneficial during these times?

Entrepreneurs can be likened to superheroes when the economy is doing bad or good. When unemployment is high, and the economy is contracting or stagnating, dynamic entrepreneurship could be a catalyst in turning the economy around. By developing novel products or increasing competition, new firms can boost demand, which could, in turn, create new job opportunities and reduce unemployment. When the economy is running well, consumer optimism increases, banks begin lending again and the entrepreneurial spirit comes alive once again.

When entrepreneurs challenge stagnating and complacent firms by providing the much-needed competition, these firms are nudged to invest more in research and development to keep up with the sudden competition. If entrepreneurs are consistently encouraged, in bad economic times as well as good, then all businesses are kept on their toes, motivated to work continuously to improve and adapt. Entrepreneurs are the fresh blood that keeps economies healthy and flourishing even as some individual firms fail.

Entrepreneurs often create new technologies, develop new products or process innovations, and open new markets which almost always lead to economic growth. Consumers benefit from the resulting lower prices and greater product variety due to the establishment of new businesses. These new businesses intensify the competition for existing businesses by bringing new products, methods, and production processes to the market and by boosting productivity and competition more broadly.

Entrepreneurship is indeed crucial to a dynamic economy. Entrepreneurs create employment opportunities and keep the ball rolling in the market.

A recurring theme in American entrepreneurship is the decline of one enterprise that will ultimately lead to the success of another company. For example, when the railroad or the biggest business sector after World War I declined, trucking became the next big business.

Another more modern example of this theme is the computer software industry. The computer software industry has seen similar changes. Apple is known to be the creator of the first operating system for personal computers. But when Microsoft substituted Apple's OS with a brand-new operating system, Windows, new concepts in entrepreneurship such as anti-trust, monopoly and copyright laws emerged. This suggests that the number of enterprise businesses have saturated many industries, leading to a heightened significance of legislature and court rulings.

Other well-known enterprises in the tech industry include Google, Facebook, and Twitter. Our ever-changing world became faster because of technology. Today's entrepreneurs have taken advantage of the unique ways in connecting, communicating, and accessing information in our technological landscape. Their products are custom tailored for consumers with specific demographics in mind. Technology, particularly with respect to transportation and communication had always been important to this nation even way back in World War I.

Now, more than ever, keeping up with the technology has become crucial for today's entrepreneurs. Web technology and online marketing are two other areas where today's entrepreneurs can keep track of important visitor information. Expertise in those areas will certainly lead to more clicks on advertisements and an increase in product sales when applied correctly. This is valuable information in increasing revenue and profit.

Numbers proves how entrepreneurship is deeply entrenched in America. According to research from Babson College and the Kauffman Center for Entrepreneurship, 10% to 17% of adults in the United States take an active role in start-ups. The Global Entrepreneurship Monitor even reported that nearly one in ten working adults in the United States, or 18.3 million, were actively involved in the process of forming or leading early stage ventures.

America's small entrepreneurial firms have been the catalyst to the country's economy growth in the past and it will continue to do so in the future. In fact, there are over 40 million entrepreneurs conducting some form of business activity in the United States. It is estimated by the U.S. Small Business Administration (SBA) that there are about 25 million small businesses, defined as companies with fewer than 500 employees. According to the SBA records, there are about 180,000 companies that have between 100 and 500 employees, and about 5.7 million companies with fewer than 100 employees. The balance—the 12.8 million sole proprietorships and the 6.4 million limited partnerships or limited liability companies—have no employees.

In their landmark book, Venture Capital at the Crossroads, William D. Bygrave and Jeffry A. Timmons dubbed entrepreneurship as the American economy's secret weapon. According to the U.S. Department of Commerce, small businesses account for nearly 60% of the gross national product, produce some 75% of new jobs, and are a major source of new technologies and innovation. It has been estimated that 18% of the financial assets held by U.S. households, or $2.4 trillion, is invested in private ventures.

According to Amar Bhide, who studied the founders of successful ventures, about 80% of the country's entrepreneurs had a college degree, 48% had a four-year degree, 15% had an MBA degree, 20% had some other advanced degree, and 11% were only high school graduates. As for their origins and backgrounds, 63% were from middle class, 26% described their backgrounds as working class, 5% were poor, and 6% came from affluent backgrounds.

Entrepreneurship can also be a source of empowerment for all. An important but often neglected, area in the study of entrepreneurship is the role of women in the building of high-growth ventures. Historically, women have tended toward low-risk, slower-growth ventures. But things are changing as women in senior levels of marketing and management are being exposed to raising money and managing new business ventures. The number of entrepreneurs is growing. Indeed, in the survey put together by U.S. Census Bureau, it was found that African Americans own more than 800,000 ventures and that there were some 3 million minority entrepreneurs by the end of the 1990s. This is not even considering the huge swell of skilled immigrants being a source of well-educated and successful entrepreneurs.

A more important question is how feasible entrepreneurship is specifically for you. Data provided by a 2015 Gallup survey report showed that suggested Baby Boomers are twice as likely to be planning to start a business within a year than Millennials. In fact, the percentage of entrepreneurs ages 55 to 64 has risen steadily from 14% in 1996 to 23%. Over that same period, median net worth for households over age 65 increased by 38%, suggesting access to capital might be less of hurdle for a greater number of entrepreneurial Baby Boomers.

Our country is still ranked top by most indexes or comparative studies that measure elements of entrepreneurial performance. Furthermore, the rise of economic stability around the world opens new investment and market opportunities for Americans.

Now, forget all the figures, facts and history presented to you. Clear your head and reflect:

Do I have what it takes to be an entrepreneur—and a good one at that?

The most important question is what are the qualities that make up a good entrepreneur?

According to Michael E. Gerber, author of *"The E-Myth Revisited"*, there are four characteristics that a person must have to become a successful entrepreneur. These four dimensions work together to drive and fuel the creation, the vision, the launching and the success of any enterprise. An aspiring entrepreneur must develop these four distinct dimensions namely The Dreamer, The Thinker, The Storyteller and lastly, The Leader. Oftentimes, one or two dimensions are far more developed than the others. To be a great entrepreneur, Gerber proposes a merging of these four dimensions by developing the characteristics that are yet to be developed.

The first dimension is probably the one most often misunderstood. The Dreamer is confused with daydreaming but these two are in fact, very different. The Dreamer has a very strong purpose for his or her big vision. This purpose drives them to make the vision come to life. This purpose is not as simplistic such as looking for a better job, earning more money and improving the quality of life. No, The Dreamer aspires to be more than that and this desire and need to be more nourishes that purpose.

The second dimension is the one that best complements The Dreamer. The Thinker serves as the cool logic to The Dreamer's burning passion. The Thinker plans, moves and directs. While The Dreamer conjures up the "what", the Thinker comes up with the "how" in achieving the "what".

Gerber's third dimension is The Storyteller. The Storyteller conveys and passes the enthusiasm and excitement of their new enterprise to others. Without the Storyteller's encouragement, The Dreamer and The Thinker's passion would eventually dim and die down. The Storyteller, therefore, serves as the voice for the passion and the method.

The last dimension that must be fully-developed is The Leader. The Leader is the one who ties everything together. The Leader puts the pieces of the first three dimensions and weaves everything together to make one coherent fabric. He or she knows what the Big Plan is, how to get there, when it will get there and what the Big Plan would look like afterwards. The burden rests upon the shoulders of The Leader to ensure that all the smaller pictures come together to make their desired big picture.

All these make up a good entrepreneur. Each of these characteristics must be functioning. When all the four aspects are working together, so does your business.

Now, assess yourself and your personality. Have you nurtured these four dimensions within you? Which of the dimensions are you the strongest at… and the weakest at? What are the steps you must take to develop the dimensions you lack?

Survey: Are You an Entrepreneur?

The road to entrepreneurship is not an easy one. Even the successful ones had asked themselves at some point in their career if they had made the right choice. We often hear the phrases, "I want to work from home" or "I want to be my own boss," when talking about motivations in starting a business. What really stands out is the phrase,

"I have a great idea and it just might be what the world needs!" Having a good idea, motivation and passion are the ingredients to an entrepreneur. But what makes an entrepreneur a successful one?

A successful entrepreneur must have an entrepreneurial mindset. They are not content on just taking orders and accomplishing tasks. No, a successful entrepreneur has a strong sense of initiative and creativity. They often think big and out of the box. They not only work hard but they are also very resilient. Giving it your 150% when you are being asked for your 110% is what makes an entrepreneur a successful one. An entrepreneurial mindset isn't found in everybody. It takes a certain, special quality found in a unique individual. An extra dash of imagination and a bit more of creativity.

Here are some questions you must ask yourself first to know if you have an entrepreneurial mindset:

Are you a risk taker?

Venturing into entrepreneurship would involve getting out of your comfort zone and exploring new ideas and concepts. It would also mean that any aspiring businessman must take risks when it comes to things they know have the greatest potential of yielding fruits.

Do you take advantage of opportunities that comes your way?

An important aspect of any entrepreneur's make-up is timing. You must be able to recognize an opportunity when it presents itself to you and seize it. It should always be "now" instead of "later" when going into business.

Are you excited about the idea of challenges?

An entrepreneur should feel fear. It helps them from being too reckless. However, an entrepreneur must also learn how to balance fear and learn to face it. Challenges and obstacles will always be there, but a good entrepreneur will not be daunted by them—instead he or she thrives under pressure. They feel the fear but doesn't let it freeze them up. They continue to move forward anyway.

Are you willing to learn?

A good entrepreneur's mantra is "learn, learn, learn." They are not afraid to learn and try out new things. They do not get offended when they are being challenged with a new concept or an idea. Instead, they learn how to stretch and adapt because they know full well that once they start their own business, they will have to do it all themselves. So, they learn as much as they can and absorb everything to expand their skill set.

Do you adapt to change quickly?

The adage that says the world is moving at a fast pace has never been truer nowadays. The technological landscape is constantly mutating and transforming. In no less than two heartbeats, the technology we are familiar with has become obsolete and replaced with faster and sleeker ones. A good entrepreneur does not let themselves go stagnant. They move along with the changes. They know that they must adapt to keep up with the needs of their customers and the technology in the business.

Are you self-disciplined?

The other side of the coin in being your own boss is having no one to pressure you into working. You must be able to do what needs to be done, whether you like it or not. Being your own boss will need you to discipline yourself to meet deadlines and accomplish tasks right on schedule.

Do you enjoy sales?

There are two types of sales, Consultative and Catalyst. Those who enjoy consultative sales prefer customers find them or seek them out. Catalyst sales are for those who enjoy the hunt, seeking out customers. Sales is the pepper to business' salt. They always go hand in hand. Neither can exist without the other. You must truly enjoy sales for you to go into business. Learn everything you can about it until you are comfortable with it. Loving what you sell is one of the core ingredients of enjoying sales.

Are you influential?

Having influence that can attract people to you. There are already many businesses that offer the same things you are offering. That is the cold, hard truth. The way to success is to stand out from the pack with your personality and influence not just on social media but also in real life.

Are you a connector?

Networking is one of the greatest things you can do for yourself. Having connections, you can refer to can open doors not just for you but for others as well. Having a strong set of connections will help you in the long run.

Are you results-oriented?

You must know and differentiate between your short-term and long-term goals. You should also have concrete plans on how to achieve them. By having a plan for achieving those goals, you will be able to measure your successes for you to move on to bigger goals.

Do you understand the intrinsic motivational factors?

Understanding human nature is highly important. When you know what drives a person, you will have a deeper understanding of how to attract people and close sales. Having a knowledge of these motivational factors will provide you an edge over your competitors because it allows you to be smart or strategic when it comes to marketing yourself and your business to people. You will also know how to handle your employees with maturity and grace.

Are you willing to expand by hiring help and build teams?

What makes a bad entrepreneur? A bad entrepreneur thinks that they can do it all themselves. They end up doing everything and burning themselves out which will ultimately lead to failure in business. A good entrepreneur admits that they need help in handling the business and lets people in to share the workload. Welcoming new people will also allow the culture in your business to grow and not remain stagnant. New perspectives and ideas on how to face problems will be accessible to you.

If you can picture yourself having those qualities, then you just might have one good entrepreneurial mindset. However, if you are still unsure about it there are several tests that can help you determine if your personality is truly cut out to be an entrepreneur. By taking these entrepreneur self-assessment tests, you might have a clearer view of what career path to take, identify your strengths and weaknesses, hire the right people to work with and build better teams for yourself.

Learning who you are inside and out can still prove to be difficult despite living with yourself. Assessing yourself and pinpointing your qualities objectively is not an easy feat. However, using professional assessment tools can help you understand how you work best so you can make the necessary adjustments, what motivates and drives you, recognize when you are in over your head and in need of help, see holes and spots you need to improve on, and lastly, choose who to hire that meshes perfectly with your personality.

First of these tests is the well-known Myers-Briggs Type Indicator. Based on Carl Jung's theory of personality, the Myers-Briggs Type Indicator "indicates your likely patterns in gathering information, making decisions, managing your energy, and interacting with the outside world." According to Jennifer Selby Long of The Selby Group, "if you learn about your unconscious blind spots, energizers, and energy drainers, you can use this knowledge to gain an edge over your competitors".

It is important not to just use one evaluative tool. In fact, Malcolm Munro of Total Career Mastery advises, "The danger of using just one tool and getting just one opinion is that a person's hard-wired personality is just one dimension of what a successful entrepreneur would be. It's a good starting point, but without some advice around the results, it might mean some potential superstar entrepreneurs may not pursue the career and wannabes jump in and quickly fail."

Carol Roth, the author of the New York Times bestselling book, The Entrepreneur Equation, says that her book provides "a bevy of exercises and assessments to help you assess your personality vis-à-vis entrepreneurship, as well as your mindset, timing and the particular opportunity. When asked why personality tests are so important to a budding entrepreneur, she answers, "Sometimes it's hard for someone to see the forest through the trees. [Self-assessments] help individuals get in touch with what their core competencies are and how those may overlap with what's needed to take on running a business.

And while personality is involved in your success, it's not the only defining factor. Timing always plays a role, she says. "You may be averse to financial risk currently, but that's something you may be able to overcome if you saved up enough prior to opening a business. Not all the characteristics are static."

There are so many personality assessment tools available for you to use. These evaluating tools provide profound insights as to who you are as an entrepreneur and a person. The results from these assessments will arm you with the right tools to grow and nourish, strengths to develop, weakness to improve on and direction when considering a change in your career path. But the best part of these tests is helping you answer that burning question, "Am I suited for entrepreneurship?"

Chapter 6

The Five Stages of a Career Transition

The career transition, especially for senior executives, is challenging. Senior executives often experience varying stages of transition. After all, they get to do things they haven't done for many years such as look for a job. Our current economy helped narrow down hundreds of job openings to a handful. Senior jobs became few and far between. Today, companies want to increase productivity with less headcount.

Executive Baby Boomers are one of the largest generations moving out the workforce today. These are some of the stages Baby Boomers tend to experience when they are once again out in the market.

1. Consider retirement
2. Continue search for a traditional job in their field of expertise
3. Start their own company
4. Buy an existing company
5. Buy a franchise

Let us take a closer look at each of these steps.

The first option is to consider retirement. It was Otto von Bismarck, a conservative minister president of Prussia, who introduced a radical idea to the Reichstag. He proposed that the government should provide financial support for the older members of the society — retirement, for short. Retirement was considered radical back then. The norm was people working until they die. That's just the way life was. You were either breaking your back on a farm or, if you were well-off, managing a farm or a larger estate until your time is up.

Von Bismarck was motivated by his socialist opponents to make better living conditions for the people in his country. He argued to the Reichstag that "those who are disabled from work by age and invalidity have a well-grounded claim to care from the state." While it took nearly a decade, German government eventually created a retirement system. This system provided for citizens over the age of 70 — given that they live that long.

This system was still not fully developed and has several flaws. That retirement age just about aligned with life expectancy in Germany then. Even with retirement, most people still worked until they died. There were exceptions to that rule though. Military pensions had long been given to soldiers who had risked their lives (though those pensions didn't necessarily mean they could stop working altogether). In the United States, starting in the mid-1800s, certain municipal employees — firefighters, cops, teachers, mostly in big cities — started receiving public pensions, and in 1875, the American Express Company started offering private pensions. By the 1920s, a variety of American industries, railroads, oil and banking were promising their workers some sort of support for their later years.

These pension programs had marked the age of 65 as the proper retirement age. Some researches had shown that there was a decline in mental capabilities starting around the age of 60. These results were further fueled by the conventional wisdom that by the age of 60, a man had most certainly done his part and must pass on the burden to the younger generation. When the federal government started creating what would become Social Security, some of the policies suggested had workers off the clock at 60, or even earlier. The economics of that didn't quite work, though, and so when the Social Security Act was passed in 1935, the official retirement age was 65. Life expectancy for American men was around 58 at the time.

However, that soon changed when the Great Depression ended, and Americans started living longer due to better medicine and economy during the post-war. In 1960, life expectancy in America was almost 70 years. Suddenly, more people were living past the age where they had permission to stop working and the money to do it. Finally, they began to retire in large numbers allowing them to stop working and embrace a life of leisure and golf. For a few decades, older Americans had eventually stopped working at a certain point which had given the next generation the impression that they should also be able to retire, further normalizing the retirement culture we have today. The Social Security

Administration estimates that there are 38 million retired people in the United States alone.

But what does the word "retirement" even mean? The term "retirement" is a misnomer. Retirement is essentially a tax-advantaged savings or invested funds that you can't tap until you are well, retired. The fund isn't for "retirement," as such. It's a fund that lets one legally avoid or defer taxes on their investment, in exchange for their promise that they won't spend the money until they've reached the full retirement age.

Another thing about retirement is that it doesn't always happen by choice. Sometimes people are forced into an early retirement because of recession, industry decline, age discrimination, health issues, family care and many more. The recessions weaken the economy so much that it forces employers to lay off even the best workers. Companies must make that tough call due to declining revenue—even if that means firing their great workers.

Technological change can make some industries and careers obsolete. Many people in the newspaper industry, for example, felt the pinch after the popularization of the Internet. When classified ads transitioned from print publications to Craigslist and other websites, newspaper revenue dried up—taking plenty of jobs along with it.

Age discrimination in the workplace can be very hard to prove but many older workers have complained about discrimination because of their age. The fact is, some employers tend to view older workers, however unfairly, as less-technologically-advanced than their 20-something counterparts. This can make finding a new job difficult, especially if discrimination is combined with industry decline or a recession. The competition can be a lot steeper than usual.

Health issues can also drive people to early retirement. Even if some retirees would prefer to keep on working, sometimes they find that their health might not be in tip top shape anymore. As we age, the risk for deteriorating health also increases. This condition might significantly impact our ability to work.

Other people find themselves forced to retire early because a family member needs long-term care. Paying for a full-time stay-at-home nurse could cost more than your annual salary, so it makes the most financial sense to retire from work to care for your family yourself.

In March 2017, Merrill Lynch Finances in Retirement Survey revealed that the average cost of retirement had risen to $738,400. According to Fidelity's Retiree Health Care Cost, $260,000 of that number will go to healthcare costs alone. $738,400 may be the average but retirees accustomed to high incomes may need even more than this to maintain their standard of living in retirement.

Most retirees expect to see their expenses drop when they retire hence the standard recommendation that retirees will need 70%-80% of their pre-retirement income. But the quality of life we want during retirement makes the amount of income we need vary. If you plan to live a simple life and settle down in your already paid off home, then 70% of your current income is probably just enough to get by. On the other hand, if you want to live the high life in retirement, taking trips and indulge in luxury, then it is safe to say that you will be needing more than 70% of your pre-retirement income to have the retirement you want and deserve.

Granted, some day-to-day expenses will decline or perhaps, disappear once you retire (i.e. auto expenses, monthly housing payment if house is already paid off), However, healthcare expenses might be a completely different story. Healthcare is the one expense that tends to rise throughout your retirement. Let's face it. The older we get, the more chances we have of getting sick and needing more medical help to stay healthy. And boy, does medical help costs a bundle.

The $260,000 healthcare finding from the Fidelity study assumes that retirees will have the traditional Medicare coverage, but it doesn't include long-term care expenses. In fact, the Fidelity study further shows that a hypothetical retiring couple of 65 years of age would need an additional $130,000 for long-term care insurance and that is assuming they are in good shape.

The average retirement age in the U.S. is 63 years old but a recent survey by human resources consulting firm Willis Towers Watson posits that 70 years old is becoming the new target retirement age. In a recent survey by CareerBuilder, it was shockingly found that almost a quarter of Americans believe they won't be able to retire until the age 70. Worse yet, 5% are convinced they'll never be able to retire at all. A frightening one third of Americans, majority are 55 and over, admit to having no retirement savings whatsoever.

However, as mentioned earlier, retirement is not always going to be a choice. There are several factors that can trigger early retirement such as recession, industry decline, age discrimination, health issues and other personal reasons.

The second option is for those who cannot afford early retirement. It is looking for another job in the same industry. Working longer actually has its perks. By working longer, you are provided with more opportunities to save up for retirement. Not only, that but working longer shortens up the number of years you spend in retirement which can help make your savings go further. But looking for another job has its own set of problems too. Job hunting is hard enough as it is—try job hunting with even more odds stacked against you. High end jobs are hard to find or to duplicate. The search takes longer which, in turn, raises the level of frustration even more. In this good economy, it is even more tough to ask for the high salary you are accustomed to since the competition nowadays is a lot steeper with younger counterparts who are willing to work longer for lesser pay.

At first, you will be confident. You had been a great manager in your old company. You had achieved so much and worked your way to the top. That ought to speak for itself. You are confident that you will get accepted to another job soon. It is only a matter of time. While losing your job made you feel embarrassed you are still confident that you can land your next job in no time. You are used to making very important and big decisions.

Consider this. You are more than likely competing with younger people, sometimes even half your age, for the same jobs. There are instances where employers prefer hiring younger candidates for the job since they have more energy to do more work with lesser pay. Social media and LinkedIn profiles have become a must. In fact, a recent study by the Society for Human Resource Management found that 77% of employers are using social networks to recruit, a sharp increase from the 56% who reported doing so in 2011. Among the recruiters using social tools, 94% said they use LinkedIn.

The truth is, you haven't had to show anyone a résumé in years. The old résumé that got you your old job wouldn't be as good and effective today. You start to update and compile a new résumé that you think will convince your potential employers that you are an award-winning, a rock star of an employee. Every recruiter/employer is looking at "Key Words" as part of their search. Key Words are words that describe an attribute that the seeker is interested. Sadly, most people tend to just think about their own perspective and not necessarily the HR Director's. While your awards may mean a great deal to you, if they do not fit with what is being asked for in the job listing, they probably won't matter much today.

You begin to discover that there are skills such as day-to-day administrative tasks, organization, details, logistics that you have no idea how to do. With an already steep competition in place, companies would most likely choose those who already know how to do certain tasks to maximize efficiency instead of taking the time to train a new employee. Sometimes you begin to encounter the term "technology impaired" and to your shock, this phrase is repeatedly used to describe you. When did the world change so much?

This is when doubt begins to set in. You start to think that this may not be as easy as you once thought it was. In fact, maybe this will take a lot longer than what you originally had in mind. Suddenly, you are 27 weeks in and you still haven't found a job. Not only does this sink your morale further but fear begins to creep up on you. Fear of not making ends meet because money is about to run out soon.

It is starting to dawn on you that there is a higher barrier of entry than what you were expecting. It has proven to be more difficult to get through the senior executives' gatekeepers. Jobs you are eyeing are already filled. Staff members that have been paying their dues for years at the company are already in line to get the coveted top jobs. Another factor is that companies do not want to take risks in bringing an outsider into such an important position. Employers most definitely do not want to spend money in conducting a search for an outside senior executive, favoring internal candidates instead.

Fear starts to leave an acrid taste in your mouth. You start playing mind games with yourself. Having come from a high paying job, it is natural that you would want your next job to pay equally as well. But you soon find that the more desirable the position is, the more people there are fighting for it. Fear clouds your judgment which hinders you from taking on that challenge.

Having gotten used to a big lifestyle with bigger bills that your previous salary can cover, you realize that you might not be able to afford the kind of life you are used to having. You might be forced to take on a simpler and less extravagant way of living. Insecurity begins to blossom. Your failure seems greater because you were higher up on the corporate ladder before you lost your job. You are not being taken seriously as a job candidate.

There is also the dreaded age discrimination. Let us acknowledge it. No matter how progressive we think we are, there still exists the concept of age discrimination. You find yourself being perceived as too old by employers. Companies fear that you won't last long at the company and they have concerns about investing in you. Most will think that you may be "too expensive" and not worth it because they doubt that you will be able to keep up with a fast pace or have the necessary technology skills to thrive in their working environment.

From that insecurity stems hopelessness. You lost all that confidence making you consider the horrifying option of not getting another job and forcefully retiring earlier than planned. You keep sending out resumes, go on interviews, spending all your extra time networking and yet nothing seems to be happening. Bills are piling up and money is running out. Your confidence took a hit. Doubts and fears begin to plague you alongside insecurities. You begin to see yourself as old and unable to compete with your younger counterparts. You begin to make compromises and start to lower your asking price. You are asking for almost half or even a third of what your previous salary was.

All that despair will eventually lead to inertia. Inertia is defined as the tendency to do nothing or to remain unchanged. *"I don't have what it takes to do what I want."* You start to believe that you cannot do this. You get stuck with feelings of frustration that you are not living up to your potential or doing meaningful, enjoyable work, which causes you more pain and isolation. You look around and see other people thriving, succeeding, and making impossible dreams happen. You become so frustrated that you remain in a state of inertia—unchanging and unevolving.

Gender bias in the workplace is something all professional women are hyper-aware of, and age discrimination lawsuits are becoming more common as the baby boomer population ages. Some women senior executives feel their gender and age are working against them when looking for jobs. They feel discriminated not just for age or for gender, but for both. Women over the age of 50 are finding it very difficult to get hired even if they have more than adequate experience. In fact, experience is posing a significant hindrance in their job search. Studies show that employers are less likely to request interviews from women over 50 than those between 35 and 50 with the same amount of experience.

A glaring difference between men and women is that men apply for a job when they meet only 60% of the qualifications, but women apply only if they meet 100% of them. This finding comes from a Hewlett Packard internal report, and has been quoted in *Lean In*, *The Confidence Code* and dozens of other articles. It's usually invoked as evidence that women need more confidence. As one Forbes article put it, "Men are confident about their ability at 60%, but women don't feel confident until they've checked off each item on the list." This proves that women need more confidence and empowering.

Job search for senior executives is a long, hard and frustrating ride. Stages of transition are harder for female executives ages 50 and above since, first and foremost, they are pitted against the archaic discrimination of not only age but gender also. Compared to their male counterparts, they do not have enough confidence to begin with. Older female executives are, therefore, more susceptible to doubting themselves before they even began.

It is a fact that women are more selective and will only apply for jobs that they think suit their skills and personality and fit 100% of the requirements for. Men are not influenced by the use of masculine and feminine traits in the job description but women are commonly discouraged by usage of masculine terms such as 'assertive', 'independent' or 'aggressive' in the job description. They are much more likely to respond to terms such as 'dedicated' or 'responsible'. This stark difference plays a big role regarding stages of transition in a job search.

The third option is to start your own business. What you choose to do with the retirement money when you turn 60 is completely up to you. Plenty of older executives have launched successful enterprises. Harland Sanders, the founder of KFC, was 65 when he began franchising his business. Ray Kroc, the founder of McDonalds, was 52 when he teamed up with the McDonald brothers, his business partners. The bottom line: having money allows you to take career risks you otherwise wouldn't be able to take. When you're in your 60s, with 40 plus years of experience and tons of connections at your disposal, you might want to capitalize on opportunities. A strong retirement fund will allow you to do just that.

The fourth option is to buy someone else's existing business. The business is already up and running so you may be able to start doing business immediately, with vendors, customers, trained employees, and cash flow on day one. You will also avoid all the issues of choosing a location, building out a site, and reviewing demographic studies. An existing business has a history. Instead of guessing whether your new business will be successful, you can analyze actual historical financial data to determine whether it is a good business or not.

The fifth and last option is to buy a franchise. This option is the most viable career option for corporate employees who have experienced downsizing or unfavorable work conditions. There are four main reasons for this. Executives who are between the ages of 45-65 are looking for these key components when considering own a business.

1. They are financially risk adverse. They understand that to own a business it will take capital, capital they had earmarked for retirement. They are concerned about investing wisely as there is not enough time left in their career to recoup any losses should the business not be successful.

2. They want speed to market. They are at an age where they are within reach of retirement are wanting to have the business up and running and show a good return on their investment as quickly as possible. They also recognize they

are not 20 years old and they need to exchange their wisdom to offset their reduced energy.

3. The want to capitalize on their executive experience. They don't want o start at the bottom. The franchise model by design is looking for executives who understand how to operate and

   grow a business.

4. They don't want to go this alone. They have become accustom to working with and developing successful teams. In the franchise world the saying goes like this." You are in business for yourself (meaning you indeed own the business) but not by yourself. Immediately upon purchasing a franchise you are joined by the support of the corporate office and teamed up with the multitude of others who own the brand from around the country.

The pros to buying a franchise include franchise support, benefits from having an already established brand name, access to lower inventory prices compared to independent businesses, and easier staff recruitment. The franchise system is a proven system for operating the business and generating profits. If you are willing to pay a little more, but get to profitability quicker, then a turnkey franchise should be considered. Buying a franchise offers the opportunity to share your challenges with other entrepreneurs who are facing or have faced the same problems. As franchise companies state, you're in business for yourself, but not by yourself.

These five options all have definite pros and cons that must be weighed in. It would be wise to choose the path that can fit your personality, work ethic, financial status and of course, can give the greatest benefits suited for your goals.

Chapter 7

The Job Search

John Smith wakes up in the morning and tries not to stare too long at the ceiling. He gets up, brushes his teeth and tries not to think too much. He dons his crisp business suit, gingerly combs his thinning gray hair neatly and looks in the mirror. He puts his contact lenses in not only to see better but to hide the deadened look in his eyes. John breathes in and dusts off the non-existent dust in his already immaculate suit. He glances at himself and thinks, "I am credible and trustworthy. I am going to get hired today."

Six months ago, John was well on his way to retirement. He was secure in all the ways he thought a person must be secure. He had a high-paying, stable job that supported his family well. He loved working in the company he had been with for decades. He had his every day work routine down to the tiniest detail. He had helped the company achieve so many great milestones throughout his career. He was confident in thinking that he was one of the best. He was valuable. In just a few short years, either he would get promoted or he can retire for good. God knows that he could use a good, solid vacation. He was owed one. Everything was going smoothly until that fateful day. It was a bright Monday morning that in no way warned John for what's about to come. The phone rang. It was only a 30-minute call that felt like a lifetime. He had been fired. Just like that, John's life started to unravel.

After more than 27 weeks of job search, John's confidence starts to wane, but he is a proud man. He just must have the right job posting, the right connection, and the right timing. It is always, "I'll get the next one" until the "next ones" had begun to pile up and John still found himself jobless.

Even in this strong economy the job market had not been kind to older workers. Many are struggling in a largely digital job search process that is vastly different from what they have experienced before. John is no different. John had entered the workforce straight from high school, earning steady promotions and salary increases. While John had painstakingly clawed his way to middle management, he had no reason to update his resume in years. John had seen colleagues get laid off one by one but while he felt a slight shiver of fear, it had never dawned on him that the downsizing of his company can affect him too. Not me, he used to say. I'm valuable.

Now John is here, sending resumes left and right, with none of his prospective employers calling him back. Many recruiters these days only want e-mail applications and refuse to take phone calls. John finds himself lost in the world of LinkedIn and Facebook for networking. Stark realization sets in that his stellar resume with all his prior work experience might not be so stellar after all in the job market today.

John finds the competition getting greater in the market with competition comprising of young professionals who are even younger than his kids. Tech savvy millennials with boundless energy are what the employers deem as "less expensive." The job hunt had become a brutal experience—something John had not expected to ever experience again. But it did, with all the force of a battering ram. Having spent years building up stellar credentials and largely defining himself by his career, the ego-crushing inactivity of unemployment and continuous stream of rejection were becoming unbearable for John. Each morning, John, to his horror, finds his soul getting smaller and smaller.

The daily hunt begins around 7 a.m. in his tidy home office, where John scans online job leads. He admits he isn't a whiz with computers. Administrative assistants at his previous post handled it all that. Many positions now require computer literacy and other technological skills that he's trying to master with help from friends. It's not that John didn't want to learn. It's just that he's never needed it before. There had not been any dinners where John was not playing mind games with himself—doubt and fear plaguing his every thought.

John knew he had the skills and the talent. After all, had he not helped his past company get where it is now? Had he not thrived in that workplace for years? But gone are the days of cornering an executive in an elevator and pitching yourself in person. It is as if all the rules John had known had been thrown out the window and replaced with new ones written in a language John couldn't even begin to fathom.

Over the course of his seemingly never-ending job hunt, John has blown through a large sum in his retirement savings to cover his mortgage, living expenses and the rising cost of healthcare. He has retreated from his large social network, save for the occasional Saturday-morning coffee with friends. The sunny mask is starting to slip.

During the countless job interviews, John finds himself wrongly perceived as overqualified, overpriced, technologically challenged, and inflexible. There are even whispers of "over-the-hill" that John refused to acknowledge but creeps up in his thoughts more frequently nowadays.

John tried to compromise and started asking for half the salary he was getting in his old position. He had to do something to get a job, any job, even if he had to sacrifice his integrity in the process. But that didn't work. Some recruiters assumed that because John is vying for jobs that pay less than his previous position, he is bound to jump ship as soon as the economy improves.

John soon found out that no matter how desirable he was at 28, he was no longer a hotshot at 57. Most of the recruiters will only give a cursory glance at his resume, dismissing him altogether. Who cared about his life story and how he got there?

A poisonous thought begins to grow in his mind like a weed. Am I past the unspoken cut off age? No matter how much they say age discrimination isn't happening, deep in John's gut, he believes that it still thrives anyway. All that John wanted was an opportunity to prove himself again, that he wasn't as old as what these recruiters think of him as.

John started to apply for jobs online. He applied for jobs with descriptions that exactly matched his resume. But John soon began to learn that "You're too old" can mean the same thing as "You are overqualified." And he had been hearing a lot of "you're overqualified" getting tossed his way for months now.

John had worked for a marketing company for years. But with his two daughters going into college, he knew he needed a higher income. His expenses have risen dramatically. The only solution he could think of is to deplete his savings to make ends meet for now. While John had not expected to be facing this, always envisioning that he'd be a lot more stable at this point in life, he considered himself still lucky for having a tough spirit.

John spends 50 hours a week job hunting. He wears a dress shirt and tie and carries business cards everywhere. He never turns off his phone. He checks his car's tank each night to be available to recruiters for job interviews. What he won't do is give up. His saved money is running out but giving up still isn't an option. Occasionally, grief would creep up on him at night. When the TV goes off and the lights go down, the quiet amplifies the fear-laced thoughts in his mind. He pushes these thoughts back night after night but every time they go back, they are twice as loud making it hard for him to shut them out. So, each morning John would wake up and try to think positively otherwise the agony would crush him. And every day, he finds it a tad bit harder to conjure happy thoughts.

John Smith exists in every 55 and older executives who want a job but can't find one. The job search can certainly be frustrating and agonizing for older workers. Every day is a constant struggle of sending out resumes and praying fervently that the stars align, and you land a job. The frustration of not landing a job can break one's spirit but you should never in a million years give up. Instead, channel that frustration and pent-up emotions into something productive. Stay focused and never waver. Crisis can be blessings in disguise that might provide a solution that will help you achieve your long-term goals sooner than you'd expect.

Chapter 8

Owning your own business

When going into business, one might automatically assume that the only choice is to begin from scratch, brainstorming new ideas and building everything from the ground up. That doesn't have to be the case. For executives who want to transition from the corporate world to entrepreneurship, it is more beneficial to buy an existing business or a franchise for these two business models pose less risks than start-ups. You will have the blueprint of a tested and proven operation that will serve as a guideline. For novices in entrepreneurship, this can make all the difference in the world.

Buying a business or a franchise are often more expensive than startups. But one mustn't forget that it is a lot easier to get financial assistance in buying an already established name than in starting a completely new business. Why is that so? It is because bankers and investors feel more secure to lend money when proposed with a business that already has a proven track record. So be sure to opt for the course of action that is less risky with easier access to working and starting capital and higher success rates.

Not only that, but an existing business or franchise will guarantee you an established customer base, reputation and employees who are familiar with all aspects of the business. Plus, an already existing business will most likely have equipment and inventory, location (and by any chance, it might still have few years remaining on the lease), employees (with a few promising ones you might want to keep), customers who are familiar with your brand, and a track record where you can look at the business' books, records and tax returns and get some sense of how much money you will make. For beginners who wanted to try out entrepreneurship for themselves, having access to these will be a great help in acquainting themselves with the business.

Before you get all excited, do take note of the distinction between buying an existing business and buying a franchise. These two are completely different business models. Before committing yourself to anything, you must first know everything about these two to know which business model fits your personality and goals the best.

It all begins in the boardroom. Let's take look at a comparison between Starbucks and Dunkin Donuts. Both are very successful businesses. One is a franchise and the other is not.

Starbucks chose not to franchise their business based upon their desire to have total control over their operations. They were willing to invest their own capital and hire enough staff to build an organization that will support their growth. They have become very successful. On the other hand, the executives at Dunkin Donuts sat in their boardroom and decided to franchise their operation. Their thinking was, that it is better to use other people's capital, for a buyer who has skin in the game will be more invested in the success of the company than an employee would be. In implementing this strategy, they have defined parameters for choosing who they will sell their brand name and secrets to. They are specifically looking for executives who have a good business acumen along with the needed capital to invest. They too have become very successful.

Both models work equally well. However, the franchise model is designed specifically for executives.

To refresh, a franchise is a business model where the business owner or franchisor sells the right to their business logo, name and model to an independent entrepreneur or the franchisee. In business format franchising, the franchisor and the franchisee have an ongoing relationship. The franchisor gives access to services like site selection, training, product supply and marketing plans. The most enticing part about franchising is purchasing the rights to use the name, logo and products of a larger and already established brand. Having said that, you will be able to enjoy the perks such as brand recognition, promotions and marketing. However, it also means you will have to follow specific guidelines from the parent company about running your business, lessening your freedom by a fraction. If you are the type of person who thrives working within a system, then this will not be a problem for you.

On the other hand, buying an existing business basically means just that. Once you buy an already established business, you take full ownership of the business. The main advantage of this business model is the existing blueprint that contains important details such as customer base, operating expenses, and even fully-trained employees. You might have more freedom in this business model but unlike a franchise, the risk is yours alone to face with no support from a parent company. Without the set vision, infrastructure and external guidance a parent company can offer, you must face more trial and error when it comes to figuring out the most efficient way to run your business.

For older executives who had been in the corporate world for many years, buying a business or a franchise is the way to go. However, even in this great economy, you must still be vigilant when it comes to choosing the right business or franchise to invest in. There are many factors you must consider in making sure that you have the best deal possible when investing. Here are some factors:

First things first. You must choose the right type of business for you. That means going into something you know you can commit and give yourself 110%. There are many businesses out there to choose from. Before you get overwhelmed, narrow down the scope. Look into businesses that are in the industry you have knowledge of and are passionate about. Contemplate the kind of business that, not only are you interested in, but absolutely matches your expertise and experience. Consider the size of the business you are looking for and can handle, the geographical location, the labor pool and costs of doing business in the area you have chosen, and the wages and taxes that come along with it. See how the list of businesses grew shorter and less overwhelming? Now once you have chosen the area and the industry you would like to get into, investigate every business in that region that meets your requirements. This can be done by looking in the local newspaper's classified section under "Business Opportunities" or "Businesses for Sale". You can also run your own "Want to Buy" ad describing what you are looking for. Also, do not be discouraged if a business you see a potential in isn't for sale. There is a chance that the business owners might consider selling when given an offer. This is where your networking abilities, business contacts and influence come into use.

In choosing the right type of business that will suit your financial capabilities, talents, expertise and personality, another advantage would be contacting a broker or a franchise consultant. Having a franchise consultant or a business broker that prescreens a business for you to make sure you avoid bad business risks, helps you identify your interests and focus your skills to a business, negotiates for you and assists you with tons of tedious paperwork will be invaluable for those first-time buyers.

Speaking of brokers and franchise consultants, it is also important to put your acquisition team together. By team, it means getting not only a broker or a franchise consultant but also an attorney, a banker, an accountant to help you. These advisors will provide wise counsel according to their respective fields. They will be able to guide you through proper due diligence. This preliminary analysis will consist of asking why the business is being sold in the first place. There has got to be reason. Your trusted advisors are the ones who will help you get to the bottom of things to prevent bad business deals. Does the business control enough market share to stay profitable? Are raw materials needed in abundant supply? How has the company's product or service lines changed over time? How is the community changing? Is the population increasing or declining? Is the population getting older or younger? All these demographic and political changes can greatly affect the business. You will have to assess the company's reputation and the strength of its business relationships by talking to existing customers, suppliers and vendors about their relationships with the business.

After the analysis, if the business continues to look promising, your acquisition team would move forward to examining the business' potential returns and its asking price. Business owners and/or accountants will present projected financial statements upon your request. Your team will review the balance sheets, income statements, cash flow statements, footnotes and tax returns for the past three years to determine the business' health. These documents will help you conduct a financial analysis that will spotlight any underlying problems and provide a closer look at a wide range of less tangible information.

Before deciding to buy a business or a franchise, make sure that you have checked the business' inventory, furniture, fixtures, equipment, building, copies of all contracts and legal documents, tax returns for the past three years, sales records, the complete list of liabilities, debt disclosure, merchandise returns, customer patterns, marketing strategies, advertising costs, price checks, reputation of the business, list of current employees and organizational chart, insurance, product liability, industry and market history and lastly, location and market area. It is quite a list and can tend to be a bit overwhelming. To avoid getting in way over your head, always have your trusted advisors with you when considering every nook and cranny of the business or franchise you are planning to buy. It might sound tedious, but scrutiny is always a must when a substantial amount of money is at stake.

After all that has been checked out and you are confident to buy that business or franchise, it is now time to decide upon the fair price of the business being sold. While the owner can have an idea of how much their business is worth, the figure they have in mind might differ from the figure in the buyer's mind. Each party is coming from a different perspective and usually the one who is best prepared will have the most leverage when the process enters the negotiating stage.

Since price can be very hard to really pin down, the responsibility can sometimes rest on the buyer's shoulders. The buyer must know that businesses sell for a higher price when the economy is going great and for a much lower price during recessions. Another thing to consider is the seller's motivation. Just how badly do they want to sell and why? In the chance that the seller might have personal financial problems, buying the business at a discount rate might be easier if you play the waiting game. Be sure not to show how badly you want to buy the business so that you keep the upper hand.

To recap, here are the things you must look for when planning to buy an existing business or franchise: a business that suits your interest and expertise, a good acquisition group to help you do your due diligence well, a fair price for the seller and the buyer. Follow this guideline for you to be able to make smart business decisions.

Start Ups Versus Franchise

You know that you are an excellent candidate for franchising if you thrive in working within a system. The franchise model's main premise is that it is already an established success. What does that mean? The franchisor already has a proven and tested method of doing the most efficient business. For an aspiring business person, franchising is the easiest way to transition into business ownership. A franchisee is responsible for the day-to-day business operation but she or he can always rely on the parent companies' operational support, training and marketing.

Another indicator that you'll do well in the franchising world is that your mindset is geared towards winning immediately. An added perk beyond a franchise's proven model of success is its brand awareness. You don't have to start from the ground up since there is already an established brand which means that customers are more likely to be familiar with your products and services. You have loyal-to-the-brand patrons coming right in your door in no time. For executives 55 and up, investing in a franchise with an already strong branding makes the most sense.

There are over 3000 franchises available in the country. If you are someone who prefers to find a business that will suit your needs, skills, passion and life goals than completely starting anew, it shouldn't come as a surprise that you might be leaning more towards a franchise business model.

With a successful blueprint already in place, you'll find that if you operate a store successfully, you are most likely to succeed at operating multiple stores in franchising. If you are someone that finds that scalability appealing, franchising is the thing to consider.

Lastly, if you are not that ready to leave the workforce just yet while trying your hand at business, there are several semi-absentee franchises worth exploring. You see, this type of franchise model will enable you to work on your business for 10-15 hours a week, allowing you to keep your full-time job until you are completely ready to leave it for good.

However, if you are none of those things and you prefer the complete freedom to do things your way, a start-up might just be the way to go for you. In a start-up business model, you get to do even the tiniest detail in your business your own way. In franchise model, you have specific guidelines you must follow. Note, however, that you must already have a solid plan about your business with concrete steps on how to achieve your goals if you are thinking about a start-up since you wouldn't have the support of a parent company and its reliable operations model. Also, you must be prepared to handle a lot of learning curves since all the problems in the business is yours and yours alone to fix without a franchise's giant safety net.

After assessing your personality and goals, the second thing you must look at is the success rate of each business model. Investing in a business is certainly no laughing matter. With thousands, if not millions, of dollars at stake, it is important to know the success rate of the business model you would like to get into.

Being a new franchise will mean association with a parent company with its tested and tried framework, support and brand awareness. It will also mean that you must purchase the rights to open a business from the main company.

Moving over to start-up businesses. Having no affiliations with a mother company, there would be no guidelines to follow which means that a start-up must be built from the ground up. A start-up business owner must create brand awareness from the scratch. The costs for independent businesses will be a lot higher with no assurance of a success. This entails that the owner must have a strong and in-depth knowledge of managing and operating a business already. The lower success rate for start-ups when compared to franchise is attributed to the lack of helpful supportive services offered by the parent company that the new franchise owners enjoy.

If you are finding yourself leaning more towards the franchise business model, it is therefore within your interest to learn more about the benefits of buying a franchise. Investing in a franchise, you get to have the right to use the franchisor's trademark, operations manuals, and even the privilege of being trained by the franchisor themselves in exchange for franchise fees and royalties. Why is this beneficial? It is because a strong and established brand identity will provide you with loyal customers already familiar with the products and/or services you will offer. This is also very comforting for beginners who are testing the entrepreneurial waters and learning along the way. There is less trial and error with its well-designed blueprint already set in place. This has also proven to be less risky given the franchises' high success rate.

The support system a franchise provides is certainly very valuable. This is the support you cannot have when starting an independent start-up business. Franchisees can have access to franchisors' services such as administrative assistance, bookkeeping, audit, quality assurance inspections, marketing support and even legal counsel. While the services can be charged separately by the franchisor, know that they are still available at minimal fees. Being a newbie, access to these services will give you an edge over your competitors. Another important thing to take note of is that your franchised business can grow along with the brand. A brand can expand and achieve stronger presence and recognition over time. A franchisee can therefore be affected by the brand's successes because of its association with it.

Lastly, it should not be forgotten that a franchised business follows the guidelines of the parent company or brand. Included in these guidelines is the Standard Operational Expectations (SOE) by which the franchisers can measure their performance. This also provides the golden opportunity of sharing and comparing experiences with business operators facing similar problems or situations.

To recap, there are two business models. At the end of the day, self-evaluation is critical in determining whether you are geared towards a start-up business model or a franchise model. If you are a person who likes to take on bigger risks, challenges and obstacles, is very passionate and innovative, then start-up may just be your cup of tea. But if you are a systematic person who has an appetite to grow and flourish under a successful brand name and trusted business model, franchising option might be more enticing. The franchise business model has higher chance of success with less risks.

Whatever your preference might be, remember that the road to success is often be paved with hardships and tough times. Always be persistent, never back down during trials and survive. The fruits of your labor will be abundant and taste sweeter than ever.

Chapter 9

The Emotional Journey of Losing a Job Later in Life

Losing a job a few years shy of retirement will be a lot more painful than losing a job at say, 25. It will hurt a lot more, emotionally and financially. Companies will put it as "downsizing", "reorganization", "re-engineering", and other terms that they hope will soften the blow. But reality often rears its ugly, unshaven head. You lost the job you've had for years. The job that not only became your main source of living but had also given you your sense of identity and self-esteem.

Whenever a stranger, a friend or a distant family member asks, "What do you do for a living?" The answer is automatic. But what happens when you can no longer have that job as the automatic answer? You are left feeling like a kite with its strings cut and continuously drifting away in the vast, blue sky. Completely and utterly lost.

Getting laid off is one of the hardest things that can happen. It is right next to the death of a spouse and divorce. Having defined yourself by your profession for so many years, it will be agonizing to pack up your desk and leave the office that had been your second home. After being loyal to that company for years, goodbyes will taste like ashes on your mouth and promises of keeping in touch will ring false on your ears. It is completely normal to feel betrayed, embarrassed and useless.

You've had so many triumphs and victories with that company but no matter how great you had been, it seems that the company can and will function without you.

And now, you are facing the unknown. You haven't faced the unknown for a long, long time. You are staring at it again. The future lurks, daunting and scary. Your head starts to fill with questions; questions you had never asked yourself for a very long time such as "How will I be supporting my family now?"

Job loss will hit the ego of the breadwinners the most. Of course, your family looks up to you for financial support. You had been supporting your family for years and you take pride in it. It had always been your role—taking care of the family and you had always been very good at it. When you can't take care of them anymore, it will leave you feeling vulnerable and afraid of the future. After all, losing a job will not only affect you but also the people around you who rely on you.

When dealing with tragedy, most of us go through the different versions of the traditional five stages of grief. Elisabeth Kübler-Ross, the psychiatrist who identified these stages, said that they're not necessarily experienced linearly, and some people might not experience them at all. They're just broad, common stages people go through when grieving. It isn't exclusive to death in the family or divorce, it can also be very much applied to sudden unemployment.

In dealing with grief over losing a job it is important to recognize these stages. By understanding the different emotional stages, you are going through, it allows you to cope and deal with emotions to avoid getting sucked into the pit of despair and hopelessness.

The first stage is denial. According to American Clinical Society, denial acts as "a buffer, initially protecting you from strong emotions, such as anger, and allowing you to continue functioning. If you anticipated your termination, you may feel relief at no longer having to work under stressful conditions." While denial can be necessary, it can also become a problem in a long run.

Here's how. You see, denial is conditioning the mind to think that your boss will ultimately reconsider or that getting laid off is just a minor and temporary inconvenience. It is also thinking that by being unemployed, you will have more time to do the things you cannot do when you are working. The bottom line is, you are emotionally rejecting the loss instead of actually facing it. By not facing the loss, you are not being honest with yourself or the cause of the job loss itself. You might not bother to look for alternative ways to support your family or perhaps even continue to spend money recklessly even though you cannot afford to do so anymore for the time being.

The second stage is anger. Anger is a very human emotion. It is natural to feel angry and can be quite necessary at times. You can be angry at your employer, the economy, co-workers, yourself or whatever or whoever is the most convenient to vent your anger on. You might just be angry at basically everyone. Add losing one's purpose to the financial strain it brings, anger is an ordinary reaction. But when anger enables you to drive away the people who had been supporting you through this ordeal, this will eventually backfire on you. Isolation during an emotionally wrenching experience such as this is never good.

The third stage is the bargaining stage. At this point, you start to criticize yourself. You start to see things that could possibly have changed the outcome of the situation if it weren't for this or that. This is where you make a bargain. If you do this, then maybe, just maybe, the universe will be kinder to you. You become harder on yourself to try to improve. Even the tiniest details must be scrutinized and perfected for the fear of not being good enough. While self-improvement is a good thing, a misdirected improvement will often cause more harm than good. Over-scrutinizing and inward criticism will only serve to lower your confidence and self-esteem even more.

The next stage is depression. Depression is inevitable when facing job loss. It helps to understand that feeling depressed is completely valid and you have every right to feel that way. After all, you are still a human being and it is completely okay to feel unhappy. Once you have allowed yourself to feel the loss, you will be able to see the bigger picture more clearly, enabling you to act in ways that will help you and your career.

Lastly, there is acceptance. Acceptance can just be denial itself. It should not be forced. It will take time to acknowledge fully what had happened, what you've experienced, your emotions regarding it, and in turn, you should also acknowledge that despite all that, here you still are—functioning through it. You should also learn to accept that it was not your fault. Your company fell on hard times, but you are still a great person with a lot to offer. You have made it past the grief and you are now again braving the unknown.

In losing a job, you should let yourself mourn and acknowledge the gut-wrenching loss. Once you do, let yourself feel the rollercoaster ride of emotions instead of bottling it all up. Don't ever engage in self-defeat and lose the what-ifs. Once you had given yourself sufficient time to mourn and heal, embrace the upsides. It's one of the few times in your life when you will be handed a clean slate and given time to re-evaluate your career. You will have the time to think carefully if you'd like to keep doing what you were doing, change fields, start your own business or even buy a franchise.

After surviving a layoff, you will learn a lot about your strengths and abilities. While you will need time to recover, remember to spend more time looking ahead and less time looking back. A job loss can be a blessing in disguise – a change that can bring you new opportunities at every turn.

Breathe and take it one day at a time. It's time to re -ignite, re-engage and re-invent yourself.

You are not done yet!

Chapter 10

Faith

Tragedy can come in many different forms. Everybody experiences tragedies in their lives at some point in time. It can be in the form of divorce, death in the family, losing a job and so many more. There are times when everything that can go wrong did and that gnawing, black pit of despair is so intense that it can swallow you whole. People react differently whenever a tragedy falls on them. One common reaction is anger. "Why?" is the question most often asked. Why me of all people? What did I do to deserve this?

What we should not forget is that single-most important and crucial promise given to us—God does not and cannot make mistakes. He is perfect and therefore knows us the best. He promises to use all the circumstances in our lives—may it be good or bad—to shape us to who we must be and fulfill our purpose on this earth. Everything has a reason. No matter how difficult things might get, know that it is not a random glitch in the universe. This tragedy serves a purpose in transforming you into a greater and stronger version of yourself.

Everyone has a right to feel angry. Your feelings should never be invalidated. You are entitled to feel angry, devastated and even, hysterical. That is, after all, part of the process. You must feel all this emotion, so you can choose to let them go after. After letting yourself confront all these emotions and having let them go, the next step must be choosing to trust God. God lets tragedies happen in our lives so that He can get our attention and get us on the right path He carved for us. We all must remember three universal truths: 1. God is perfect. 2. God knows us perfectly. 3. He only gives us things He knows we can handle and surpass. These challenging experiences are His way of teaching us how to love and trust Him more deeply. He wants us to grow stronger spiritually, emotionally and mentally. In doing so, we achieve lasting holiness which we discover to be more fulfilling than temporary, materialistic happiness. Dealing with difficult circumstances is a way of exercising our faith and eternal values.

Whenever God doesn't give what we ask for, instead of saying "He doesn't care about me", the right thing to ask is "Is what am I asking a need or a want?" Remember one of the universal truths mentioned above? God knows us the best because He made us. We can't truly know ourselves and our purpose because only God can. Our Maker molded us with his own hands, knowing our purpose in his mind. Therefore, when we ask for something that has not been given to us, it can only mean that it may not be what we need. Sometimes, we ask for things that we only think would make us happy. What God provides is lasting fulfillment and satisfaction. In doing so, He never fails to give what we need. Those needs provided to us might not be what we want in our limited perspective, but in God's unlimited perspective, He knows perfectly well what we need to be truly happy. That job might be one of the reasons for the emptiness in our hearts without knowing it. We might be so blinded by the paycheck that we fail to find our true purpose. God doesn't want us to live like that therefore He provides us with enough obstacles and challenges to redirect us to the path He wanted for us.

Facing these tragedies can greatly challenge our faith. Hope can often be a scarce commodity. It is also a contradiction because when life seems to be at its bleakest and everything seems to be going to hell, what one can only do is hope. Faith will get you through everything. God will replenish your reservoir of hope. Never forget that. When everything is dark and hopeless, all you can do is hang onto your faith and believe, then watch as your faithfulness will be rewarded with you emerging at the other end braver and stronger.

Another truth about faith is choosing to believe that our struggles are not unique, therefore, they can be surpassed, beaten and conquered. God is always there to guide and help us. We must only learn how to listen and trust. God can take any manure and grow a beautiful garden from it once we remain faithful. While it may be impossible to imagine how God can bring good out of our train wreck of a past and present failures, this is hardly a limiting factor. For God can do "immeasurably more than all we ask or imagine" (Ephesians 3:20).

Always remember that faith is like a muscle. Like any muscle, it needs to be strengthened and developed through exercise and lifting weights. Weights in life can be anything from feelings of doubt, guilt, envy and uncertainty to deep seated insecurities and difficult

81

circumstances. By exercising your faith especially in trying circumstances, you will grow stronger. When it doesn't seem as if God is with you, faith will strengthen you with the certainty that God is always there, and He would always have the best plan. Faith will guide you to a better place mentally, emotionally, spiritually and altogether, physically.

God provides the weight in the form of trials and wake up calls for you to strengthen your faith and get you in the best possible shape in meeting those trials. For example, Joey, 55-year-old, works in a marketing company. Although his job pays well and had kept his family stable and secure for the last decade, it was stressful. It made him unhappy. Once he took a good, hard look in his life, he came to a conclusion. He was sacrificing a lot for this job including his health and time with his family. What's even worse is that he doesn't believe in what he does and thinks that it does not have a major impact to the world. So, Joey says to himself, *"Success isn't what I thought it would be. I need to find out what God put me on earth to do."*

Aside from tragedies, God also uses negative feelings of discontentment and unhappiness to prod us to do something new and better with our lives. Bob Buford in his book "Half Time" provides a template on how to make the second part of our lives greater and leave a lasting legacy in this world. Another thing God uses to push us along are several big life choices that make us ask who we are and what is our purpose. For instance, Mary's two sons are off to college while her eldest daughter is starting to become her own woman and build her career. The house had become bigger and more desolate now that it's empty. Mary finds out that without her children she doesn't really know who she is and what to do with her free time. Raising her children while working had been a major source of satisfaction. Now that she has no one to take care of, there must be something bigger she can do. This certainly can't be it, can it? God has to have more plans ahead for her.

Joey's and Mary's situations are some of the circumstances that create a sense of needing to "do something" to find work that fits and brings a sense of purpose to our lives. There may be an itch that needs to be scratched or nudge for you to do something new and different. The problem, however, is that the actions people often take end up creating more confusion or getting them into jobs that don't fit them well, thus deepening their sense of dissatisfaction.

When one loses a job, that person will most likely scour the Internet for countless job postings, ask friends, colleagues and family members for suggestions and tips on what should they do for work. See what opportunities come their way. They may even take a series of jobs not only to appease the anxiety of losing a job but also to look for what fits. These actions are mere band aid solutions in making career choices. It does not prove wise in the long run.

This might end up causing you with an even bigger amount of frustration in your heart. You might hit dead ends or worse, find yourself in a job that is worse than the one you were in. Time passes by and the urge to find God's calling might fade. Having a job, no matter how much it can make one miserable in some instances, is comforting enough. It lulls you to a false sense of security and contentment. But the frustration will still grow, prompting you to ask, *Isn't He listening? Doesn't He care? Why won't He do something when all I want is to do something for Him?*

First thing you must realize is that this is a two-way relationship meaning that God will do His part and so should you. God will not stop guiding and nourishing you. Pray to God as hard as you can, as if everything depends on Him as well as work, as if everything depends on you, too. God has mercy, but hard work should come from no one but you yourself. Praying for guidance will be rendered ineffective if you will not move. God will not do for you what He wants you to do for yourself. The process of taking action steps also shapes you into the person God needs for you to be for the mission He has chosen specifically for you.

In Kevin and Kay Marie Brennfleck's book, *Live Your Calling*, they provided an outline of the series of action steps one must take to discover one's calling. According to the book, "God calls you to become the person He created you to be and to do the things He designed you to do. He will partner with you as you prayerfully move forward. This process is a spiritual journey in which you will learn new things about yourself and about your relationship with the Lord!"

There are five steps. The first one is to identify the key dimension or "puzzle pieces" of your unique God-given design. This resonates with Buford's kernel of knowledge about blending what you are good at with things you are passionate about. You must first learn what your most-enjoyed transferable skills, core values, personality traits, preferred roles, compelling interests, and spiritual gifts are. These can be assessed through life experiences, feedback from others, and from career tests and assessments.

Second, you must allow yourself to envision a God-sized calling. Most people often dream small that they unconsciously decide to merely stay afloat rather than thrive. Lack of vision, fear and everyday concerns hinder us from having bigger, spiritual goals. God calls us to embark on tasks and roles in our lives that we cannot accomplish on our own so that we can see His power at work.

Third is learning how to make good decisions within God's will for your life and gifts. Without your active participation, your calling just might not happen. Actively seeking your calling in partnership with God requires taking risks and making hard decisions. In doing so, you learn valuable lessons of making wise, biblically-grounded decisions which is an essential part of spiritual maturity.

Fourth, never be afraid to take prayerful action! A fundamental part of transforming yourself to become the person God wants you to become is to take appropriate actions that get to the place where you need to be. Tools that will help you "get going" in living your calling include developing personal mission statements, setting achievable goals that you are motivated to reach, and devising an action plan for creating the life God is calling you to live.

Lastly, identify and overcome any "calling blockers" in your life. "Calling blockers" are obstacles that hinder you in discovering and living your calling. One of the most common calling blockers is fear. It is also the number one reason most people aren't doing what God calls them to do. While fear is normal and functional when you are contemplating making changes in your life, it should not be an excuse not to take any action. God never calls us to stagnate in our comfort zones.

Tragedies are heart-wrenchingly difficult. These trials can bruise one's soul very deeply. But never fear for God has intended for these circumstances to happen and He is guiding you through it every step of the way. He plans not only to sustain your faith but also to replenish your soul and make do with His promises. After all, He loves you greatly and He made you with a greater purpose in mind.

Chapter 11

Purpose

In the book, Purpose Driven Life, Rick Warren said that we were made for a mission. However, our mission does not involve a martini, bikini-clad girls and remote tropical locations for some top-secret espionage. Our mission in this life is far more fulfilling and less James Bond.

You see, God made you to embody his spirit and likeness in this world. We are placed in this earth to fulfill the mission or purpose that God has given us. Fulfilling your life's purpose here on earth is essential in living for the glory of God.

According to Rick Warren, our purpose is the continuation of Jesus' mission on earth. To follow the footsteps of Jesus, we must continue what he has started. It is both a responsibility and a privilege to be molded and used by God.

Your purpose in life affects the destinies of other people, making it far more important than any job, achievement or goal. As Rick Warren puts it, "the consequences of your mission will last forever; the consequences of your job will not." No matter how big your salary is or how many promotions you have had, if these do not align with your purpose and put into good use, these achievements will only feel shallow and hollow.

A wise man by the name of William James once said, "The best use of life is to spend it for something that outlasts it." Salaries, properties, material luxuries will only perish over time. What we must all invest greatly on are the important things unseen by the human eye— love, faith and fellowship. These are forever. These will fill you up greater than any other material things.

What happens when we lose sight of our purpose? Most of the time, we are encumbered with the daily problems in our lives that we forget to stop and take a look at the bigger picture. We focus on achievements and job successes. We want to prove ourselves by striving to reach what we think is the height of success. We also want to provide for our family well, pay bills on time and have a roof over our heads. It is completely understandable.

But there is a moment in life when the inevitable happens. There is a point where despite having a comfortable lifestyle, everything still feels so unsatisfying. No matter how high your salary is, it still isn't enough. No matter how big your house is, it still isn't enough. No matter how up to date you are with the latest technology, it still isn't enough. Is it human nature to always want bigger, better and faster things, never to be satisfied?

It is because we are not living our life's true purpose. God uses this discontentment to nudge us towards the right path. He wisely sets us back to the right path by taking us out of our comfort zones. He does not only call us, but he wants us to go to him. He doesn't just want us to grow old, but he wants us to grow up as well. Aging, after all, is different from being wise.

For God, greatness isn't defined by power, possessions, prestige or even position. On the contrary, greatness, true greatness, is measured by how well we serve others. The world's different idea of greatness can blind us or make us lose sight of what's truly important. However, remembering that God has made you with a purpose will help you realize just how important serving others is rather than continuing to work for your own gain and still be unsatisfied years later.

A stellar example of a successful entrepreneur giving back is Blake Mycoskie. Blake Mycoskie travelled to Argentina in 2006. What he saw there was the immense hardship of children growing up without shoes. That touched him very deeply. With his desire to help, he used his economic capital and talents to form TOMS Shoes. With every pair of shoes sold by this company, a free pair of new ones will be given to a child in need. He called it One for One. TOMS had become a popular shoe brand but the most important contribution it had was providing over 60 million pair of shoes for children in need.

Mycoskie did not stop there. In 2011, TOMS Eyewear launched and had helped restore sight to 400,000 people in need. This movement spanned over 13 countries. TOMS Eyewear provided prescription glasses, medical treatments, and even sight-saving surgery with each purchase of their eyewear. TOMS has also done lots of philanthropic work such as providing safe water for 335,000 people in 6 countries with TOMS Roasting Co. and it had supported safe birth services for over 25,000 mothers with TOMS Bag Collection. TOMS had branched out from shoes to eyewear, coffee and even bags to help more and give back to the community.

The Walt Disney Company founded by Walter Disney is another example of a large and well-known corporation which practices a strong corporate social responsibility (CSR). Feeling the responsibility to give back to the people who helped make Disney the powerhouse it is today, the company's mission focuses mainly on the environment, community, labor standards, and puts a heavy emphasis on volunteerism. The Company gives to charity. One of its major advocacies was to help during the occurrence of natural disasters such as the earthquakes in Haiti back in 2010.

Disney offers free tickets to a million people in exchange for a day of volunteer service for an organization of their choice. This encouraged over one million people in the United States to commit to service efforts to volunteer in their communities.

A recurring theme in Disney's business practices is the environment. Disney strongly advocates for a good environmental education through motion pictures and television programming geared toward nature. In fact, Disney nature films, part of Walt Disney Motion Picture Studios, share compelling stories set in the natural world to immerse audiences. Of the three Disney nature films to date namely Earth, Oceans and African Cats, part of the proceeds from those films were given to help several threatened species and their habitats. This movement had planted three million trees in Brazil's thinning Atlantic Forest, helped protect 40,000 acres of coral reef in the Bahamas and conserved up to 50,000 acres of savanna wildlife corridors in Africa.

Microsoft, founded by Bill Gates and Paul Allen, and Google, founded by Larry Page and Sergey Brinn, are also examples of major companies who practice good corporate social responsibility. They succeed at not only being good corporate citizens, but also in communicating those characteristics to consumers who increasingly rely on their respective brands' reputation in making purchasing decisions and recommending products and services to others. Google most especially has been carbon neutral since 2007 and has implemented numerous environmentally friendly initiatives, including Google Green. The company was also one of the first tech employers to release workplace diversity statistics and has dedicated itself to expanding internet access, according to the Reputation Institute.

Fulfilling your purpose to serve others may it be in the form of shoes, animations or technology or whatever channel you choose will grant you everlasting peace and a strong legacy for years to come. What is deeply important is to find your passion and blend it with your own resources to give back to others. By doing this, you work not for your own gain but to fill your heart and soul with blessings of holiness, immense peace and satisfaction you had not felt in your years of quest with material success.

Chapter 12

Success to Significance

If you were to ask your 20-year-old self what success for him or her is, what would the answer be? Would it be any different from your answer 40 or so years later? For baby boomers, success meant financial stability, a high paying job, big house, big cars and the ability to partake in what society has to offer, be it gadgets, trips or any other luxuries. That meant working your way up. The fierce determination to "make it" can become so overpowering that it narrows down your vision leaving no room for anything else. There are no distractions. Just make it to that step to make it to another step until you have found yourself on top. For 40 or so years, that had been your journey—a single-minded pursuit to the top. Start at the bottom and work your way up. Hustle until you have made it, never once wondering what awaits at the top.

And then here's the conundrum. The "top" has been reached after years of hard work and relentless effort. You had finally made it. You have provided well for your family. You have a luxurious car parked in the garage of your beautiful home. Your co-workers look up to you with respect and admiration. You sleep well at night knowing that everything is well taken care of. You should be happy, right?

So why does the top still feel frustratingly unfulfilling and empty? You start to think that this might be hypocritical of you. After all, you have all that your 20-year-old self could ever desire and dream of. You've had a good run. Some people have so little and you had been blessed with so much. You start to question if you even have the right to be this unfulfilled and unhappy.

Two words linger every time before you go to bed: What now?

After achieving all the "successes," what is there left to do? Would success still mean an even bigger car, larger investments, bigger material things? Are we doomed to want more and more but in the end, never being satisfied?

Bob Buford in his book, Halftime, says that our lives are divided into two parts. Both parts are driven to achieve success. The first part focuses on possessing materialistic joys taught to us by society. That also means carving out a place for yourself in the field you have chosen for yourself and excel at. In this stage, we are all caught up in acquiring things we deem worthwhile such as nice house, expensive car etc. We wanted recognition for our hard work. We strive to achieve plaques, medals and other awards. We crave our colleagues' approval and respect.

When all the medals are won, properties bought, stomachs fed, and ego boosted, what comes next? Buford states that the search for meaning and fulfillment comes right after the first half is done. He points out that the second half of your life just might be better than the first after you have finally figured out what you want to do for the rest of your life. Time is essential in figuring it all out. In this stage, you have access to money, resources and time you did not have when you were in your 20s. In this stage, you are now able to carefully think and plan your life ahead at your own pace.

The first thing you must do is listen to that small but constant voice inside you. This takes time and practice. We are used to tuning that voice out in our quest for big, materialistic things in our life. We know for certain that while a large salary can buy nice things, it does not necessarily buy happiness and fulfillment along with it. If happiness could be bought, we would have no doubt that Amazon would be selling tons of that stuff in a blink. But, no, it doesn't.

Therefore, learn how to listen. Listen to that inner voice to find out who you truly are and to know for certain which path you want to take for the rest of your life.

For Buford's case, it took the death of his son in a drowning accident for him to take a step back and look at the bigger picture. That tragedy enabled him to pause and appreciate just how short life can be to live it unfulfilled. Tragedy, such as losing your job, can be God's way of calling you back to look for your purpose once again. Life is not any simpler for those with huge material successes. Success is also a spiritual journey. Being comfortable might have hindered you from seeking your true purpose. By experiencing devastating events in your life, your comfort zone is ripped apart to give you that opportunity to ponder and take stock of your life.

The message that Buford greatly stressed in his book was this: if the first part of our lives was dedicated in achieving materialistic success then the second part must be all about giving back to achieve spiritual success. Spiritual success can lead to the satisfaction and fulfillment that had evaded you in your pursuit for materialistic gain.

In the simplest sense, the second half of our lives must be about using the gifts we have been blessed with to serve others. It is a balance of give and take. We took and took and took during the first part of our lives and, therefore, it is only fair that we should give back for others to take so they, in turn, can give back for the next generation. The cycle lives on. In a sense, it is almost like biology. The carbon dioxide we exhale is food for the plants that provide the oxygen we inhale. Our bodies are buried, to nourish and give back what we took from this earth. Life is that beautiful.

But before serving, you must first know who you are. You begin by asking yourself two questions. First, what are you good at? Second, what are you most passionate about. Buford says that once you combine the things you are both good at and passionate about, the path to your legacy will be a lot clearer. This leads to the ultimate question: Is this the kind of legacy you want for yourself? If it is, then take the chance and do it wholeheartedly.

You would find your path evolving from the journey to success to the pursuit of significance.

Buford categorizes kinds of capital into two kinds: economic and social. Economic capital is the money and time you have acquired by working. This capital is spent on living requirements, worldly things and other luxuries. The second capital, social, is different. Social capital is the money and time you spend giving back to the community and the people who nurtured and helped you get to where you are right now. Think of it as a smorgasbord—a feast. It is a big feast where you can take whatever you want with no strings attached. However, the table must always be replenished so that it won't be empty for others who want to partake in this smorgasbord. There lies the social capital. The social capital works as something that can replenish the feast not because it is an obligation but because it is what you want to do.

The popular Christian saying, "It is better to give than to receive" can be applied to this second stage. The payoff for social capital is "blessedness." Blessedness is more potent and filling than happiness derived from materialistic joys. Think of eating junk food, filling but eventually you will get hungry again with no nourishment as compared to eating a good, solid meal packed with vitamins, proteins and all the good stuff. That is how blessedness works. You become a blessing not only to yourself and your family but also to the people in your community. The second stage of your life is transforming that economic capital with that of a social capital.

It might seem intimidating, in fact, it is truly unnerving. Changing your path from success to significance requires a good amount of leadership. Leadership in business and not as a weak sheep content to go with the flow of life. By becoming a leader, you must decide what risks are worth taking. While deciding and taking risks can be a terrifying prospect, knowing that you are not alone and that you are being guided can be a huge source of comfort. Seeking God and trusting His way can bring you peace and leave you in better shape for overcoming the risks and the challenges life will undoubtedly give you.

Buford is a strong champion of "healthy individualism." He says, "the image of a weak, wimpy follower is not supported at all in Scripture. Paul urges Timothy to be strong. He counsels him to "fan into flames the gift of God, which is in you... for God did not give us a spirit of timidity, but a spirit of power, of love and of self-discipline." (2 Tim 1:6-7) Once we embrace leadership, we must learn to be what we were made to be rather than pretend to be something we are not or spend our time being envious of others and letting our pride get the better of us by constantly comparing our achievement with others.

In the first half of our lives, the self is coiled tightly inwards. As time passes, it will only get tighter and tighter around itself. In the second half, the opposite happens. The "Self" unravels from that tightly wound spring and becoming able to nourish others. Jesus always emphasized that the cost of following him would entail sacrificing your immediate self, the much smaller one, for a larger gain. You give up decades of learning and the materialistic things you had acquired over the years to gain something infinitely larger and better. We are told that people are at their largest, most noble and virtuous when they give all of themselves for a cause.

The first part of our lives can be lonely without us noticing it. This is because everything we do is directed for our own gain. Everything we achieve can only gain significance when we put it to good use such as helping others. When we give ourselves, our gifts, our talents and our resources, you will find that helping others can help you a lot, too. When you help not because you are obligated to do so but because it is a natural, reflexive thing, you are bound to feel better. In fact, scientists have found out that helping others can be good for your health. It heightens one's overall zest for living and increases one's life expectancy. Did you know that people who are loveless, selfish and mean are not likely to live long? Giving of ourselves is offering love and love remains the only gift that multiplies when you give it away. Once you had actively decided that you are now ready to pursue significance, the single-most vulnerable question that must be asked is this—how do I give back?

Significance can be achieved by volunteering while at work or in owning your own business. The desire to have your second half become significant is a based on a mindset to do so. Many business owners find significance in the way they dedicate the resources of their company to meaningful causes or by investing in the future wellbeing of their employees.

When I ask my clients what they enjoyed most about their careers, the majority of them talk about how they enjoyed leading teams and building into their staff and working on projects that made a difference. One advantage a person has in owning their own business is that they are free to follow their dreams, desires and aspirations and make those a part of the fabric of their business.

The number one comment I hear from executives who are out of work is that they are not done yet. They still have a passion and a purpose and yet are frustrated for they are lost as to where they can put that energy into action. The second most common answer when asked "what is important in this next chapter of life", is without hesitation, "Quality of life". They are committed to find a vocation that will support their quality of life as they have defined it. In both instances, many have found that owning their own business has provided them the best opportunity to reach this goal.

Chapter 13

Mindset

"Becoming is better than being."

In her book, Mindset: The New Psychology of Success, Carol S. Dweck made one of the most relevant observations on human nature backed by years and years of her extensive research: that human beings can limit their potential or reach unbelievable heights by a single and powerful belief.

This is Dweck's incredible hypothesis: Who we are on a day-to-day basis stems from our mindset. Our mindset can mark the difference between mediocrity and excellence. It influences how we think, how we see problems, how we come about to solving these problems, how we cope with setbacks etc. While genes can determine our intelligence, skills and other attributes, it is our mindset that determines their extent and how far we can stretch our given strengths.

According to Dweck, we have two kinds of mindsets. If you believe that your capabilities are fixed and permanent, then you have a fixed mindset. In having a fixed mindset, you firmly attribute your set of skills to DNA and destiny. For instance, you believe that you are smart and strong, thanks to genetics. Viewing the world through this lens, you tend to validate the gifts that are inherently given to you instead of cultivating them. Instead of challenging your gifts, you gravitate towards easier goals so as not to challenge your firm belief. As Dweck puts it: "From the point of view of the fixed mindset, effort is only for people with deficiencies…. If you're considered a genius, a talent, or a natural— then you have a lot to lose. Effort can reduce you."

At the same time, having a fixed mindset and believing altogether that life has not dealt with you nicely, you might have little to no incentive of expending effort. It is like surrendering already before the battle has started because you are so fixed on the idea that everything is set in stone. You think you know yourself so well and there's no changing the things you believe you can do. A man who says he isn't good at art or math or dancing without even trying is a man who has a fixed mindset.

After countless experiments done by Dweck and her team, she had concluded that having a fixed mindset can be very problematic. It limits your potential to just what you believe it can be. Whether you had been given wonderful talents or not, having a fixed mindset will only serve to hinder you from achieving great successes. This works as a roadblock.

On the other hand, the opposite of a fixed mindset is the growth mindset. Having a growth mindset enables a person to believe that all our basic qualities from intelligence to strength are not absolute. They can be honed, improved and strengthened through years of practice and hard work. Having a growth mindset is believing that "a person's true potential is unknown (and unknowable); that it's impossible to foresee what can be accomplished with years of passion, toil, and training." Also, by having a growth mindset, you tend to have higher incentives of pursuing bigger and harder challenges in hopes of improving and pushing yourself further. A person with growth mindset can see the challenges as opportunities to conquer and succeed. Every obstacle is a way of flexing your muscles and becoming stronger.

A fixed mindset, for example, believes that smart people succeed. Hence, if you succeed you are smart. You pick easier problems to validate the belief that you are smart. You avoid bigger and harder problems, so you wouldn't have to face the fact that you aren't smart if you fail.

The growth mindset works the opposite. Instead of thinking only smart people succeed, a person with a growth mindset will ultimately say, "People are capable of getting smarter by stretching themselves out and taking on challenges." It is similar to weight training. You lift heavier weights until your muscles grow strong enough to lift even heavier weights. By believing in effort, loving and welcoming challenges and not just relying on natural talents, you open yourself up to more creative successes. Criticisms will not lower your self-esteem. You treat them as vitamins to make you better. Failure isn't a scary thing for you but an opportunity to do better and win bigger.

For the sake of simplifying her message, Dweck made it out as if these two mindsets are not interchangeable. It is possible to be somewhere along the middle of a fixed and a growth mindset. Your mindset will likely vary from the way you tackle different things. For example, your views on art may differ from your views on sciences. That means that whatever mindset you have in a particular area will guide the way you perceive things and act in that area alone.

Dweck writes, "It's also important to realize that even if people have a fixed mindset, they're not always in that mindset. In fact, in many of our studies, we put people into a growth mindset. We tell them that an ability can be learned and that the task will give them a chance to do that. Or we have them read a scientific article that teaches them the growth mindset. The article describes people who did not have natural ability, but who developed exceptional skills. These experiences stretch our research participants into growth-minded thinkers, at least for the moment — and they act like growth-minded thinkers, too."

By learning about the growth mindset, people can experience a shift in their perspective of who they are and what they can do. "Mindsets are an important part of your personality, but you can change them. Just by knowing about the two mindsets, you can start thinking and reacting in new ways. People tell me that they start to catch themselves when they are in the throes of the fixed mindset — passing up a chance for learning, feeling labeled by a failure, or getting discouraged when something requires a lot of effort. And then they switch themselves into the growth mindset — making sure they take the challenge, learn from the failure, or continue their effort."

Fixed-mindset people want to reach the top, even if they do not like what they are doing just to get there. However, a growth-mindset person arrives at the top as the by-product of doing what they love enthusiastically. The growth mindset does allow people to love what they're doing — and to continue to love it in the face of difficulties. The growth-minded athletes, CEOs, musicians, or scientists all loved what they did, whereas many of the fixed-minded ones did not.

If you are focused on having a growth mindset, there is no possible way of losing because losing is a concept foreign to you. The journey becomes the reward, even when things do not go as planned. Let go and enjoy the process of becoming the person you want to be. As behavioral scientist and author, Steve Maraboli said, "Once your mindset changes, everything on the outside will change along with it."

Chapter 14

Fear of Owning a Business "Get in the Game"

As the country rebounded from one of the worst recessions in history, companies of all sizes are seeing cultures quickly shift and grow. Constant change has become part of today's work. This can only mean that no one and no job is safe in this dynamic and ever shifting landscape. People are getting laid off left and right. There is simply no denying that simple and painful truth.

The several options after losing a job has been discussed in the previous chapters. Out of all the options, entrepreneurship might be the most exciting, the riskiest and probably the most fulfilling. Why is this so? It is because entrepreneurship lies in the fact that you can be your own boss. You run the show and don't have to worry about getting let go. For older executives, the fear of starting a business can be ten times more daunting. For starters, they are not as young as they once were. Being an entrepreneur will demand a lot of energy, time, commitment and resources.

Entrepreneurship is a big and terrifying idea some people choose to ignore the idea of starting a business in the back of their minds, dismissing it as madness. However, there are occasions wherein the entrepreneurial bug just simply would not let go. Having a great idea and strongly believing it to be the next big thing can push you towards

106

the direction of entrepreneurship. Venturing in business can be terrifying yet exhilarating at the same time. Think of it as skydiving but with lesser safeguards—that's what entrepreneurship can feel like to most.

The journey to entrepreneurship isn't easy. Some would rather not try at all because of the two cant's. These two cant's unsettled people that they immediately discard their entrepreneurial dreams without even examining if they are worth risking. So, what are these two "cant's"?

"I can't possibly own a business."

"I can't work for myself. I should stick to cubicles because it is familiar and safe."

Why is this so? What are the fears that these two cant's come from? Here are the common fears of starting a business:

I don't know where to start.

You have an idea, but you have no inkling whatsoever on how to make it come alive and turn into a reality. You have a set destination in mind with no idea of how to get there. The path ahead is dark and full of uncertainties. We are so afraid of making mistakes which is understandable. However, what will it be from now on? Will it be always one day or day one?

I'm not an expert.

You aren't and that is completely okay. Most entrepreneurs aren't experts to begin with. No one is expected to be an expert overnight. The most important aspect of entrepreneurship is learning. You keep on learning something new every day. You never stop learning even when you can finally wear the "expert" title.

They will think I am crazy.

Most people—and probably few family members, although they wouldn't admit it to your face—will think of you as utterly nuts. And they are completely right. Entrepreneurship is a risky business. The safest route is to work for someone else. But that still does not sound appealing, does it? It is because risk-taking is in every entrepreneur's DNA. If you consider yourself as having the makeup of a great entrepreneur, then the prospect of starting a business will be challenging but it is the kind of challenge you are willing to take on.

I cannot find funding.

Being a business owner would be a breeze if every person with an idea could waltz into a bank and receive a loan or attract an angel investor. Since this is not a dream world, entrepreneurs without investors must be resourceful in looking for other ways to start their business. Even if you don't have the necessary capital at first, you'll soon learn that a slow and steady process of building the business may be the best thing after all.

They don't believe in me.

Skeptics will be skeptics. Being an entrepreneur will mean facing a lot of critics and convincing them to have faith in you. You might be afraid of being discriminated against because of your age, gender, race and social status. Do not let these doubts bring you down. While people can still be judgmental, it shouldn't be a reason for you not to show up and deliver a strong work ethic.

Physical appearance is debatable, a solid work ethic isn't. Even if at first no one believes in you, people will learn to believe in your results. It will be tough at first but that should never mean losing faith to yourself and capabilities. Learn to bet on yourself.

What if I don't attract customers in the first place?

Starting a business is intimidating especially if there is no guarantee of loyal patrons lining outside your doors. It will be a hard journey. It takes a special kind of vulnerability and bravery to offer up yourself and your skills to the world without knowing if you are wanted or you will sell in the first place. But the joy you will find in your business might just be worth going through all that uncertainty.

I might not handle success well.

The opposite of the last one is this. Imagine that as soon as you open your store, people are lined up for blocks eager to see and partake in what you have to offer them. Does that picture scare you? Are you afraid that maybe you won't be able to handle the demands of running a successful business? You're not the only one. A study published in the Journal of Social Issues presented the theory that women believe that demonstrating success will result in social criticism. Men and women alike have fears of too much success because it can alienate them from their peers. The phrase "it's lonely at the top" still has a sliver of truth in there. But is that a good enough reason to not pursue your dreams? It shouldn't be.

I don't want to fail my family.

Starting a new enterprise is risky. Our number one priority is to secure our family and still provide for them. Venturing into business will require quite a hefty amount of risk taking. The stakes might be too high and you are afraid to fail your family. However, have you ever stopped to consider that maybe you and your family need this experience to grow closer together? That this will be a bonding moment for you and your family. That this can provide an opportunity for you and your spouse to show support for each other?

Your children would not want to see you extinguish your dreams. Speak to members of your family and assure them that their needs will not be compromised. Talk openly with them about the risks you're about to take and how it's important that you invest your time and energy into the success of this business. Prepare your family as best as you can and ask them to walk this journey with you.

What if I don't earn enough to recover the investment?

The definition of entrepreneur is all about a person who organizes and operates a business taking on greater than normal financial risks. If you happen to invest in your business and don't see an immediate return, keep working. Should you quit before you earn a profit, you'll never earn a profit. And if you do decide to quit before your business sees a profit, remember that you raised the investment capital once. You can always do so again.

There are so many things that can go horribly wrong.

It is inevitable. Everyone fails. No one is immune to failure. But winners are those who stand up again after failing. You sit down and cry for as long as you need to. Then you get back up again. Life is a series of failures. So, you do one thing you can only do. Life had not ended when you lost your job. It won't end with every failure we encounter in life because that is how we ultimately learn.

Getting back up is part of the game. When problems arise in business, this just provides you the chance to bounce back. As an entrepreneur, you most likely have what it takes to complete the game. So, don't be afraid when things go wrong. You can learn from them and become stronger than ever.

It is natural to have fears. Having fears enables us to survive. But the burning and lingering question remains. Should you start a business if you're over 55—or is it too late? While we typically think of entrepreneurs as young hotshots, the Kauffman Index of Entrepreneurial Activity reports that the percentage of entrepreneurs age 55 to 64 rose from 14.3% in 1996 to 23.4% in 2012. In the same time, the percentage of entrepreneurs age 20 to 34 dropped from 34.8% to 26.2%. In fact, the Kauffman Foundation determined that those age 55 to 64 are starting businesses at a higher rate than any other age group!

Rieva Lesonsky is a successful entrepreneur who started out late. She did not go into business at a young age. But that did not stop her. She took on the challenge and came out of it successful and braver. She shares the pros and cons she had experienced upon venturing into entrepreneurship later in life. She says that the first advantage of starting out later in life is the experience. As an older startup, you've got real-world knowledge of what works and what doesn't, how long things are likely to take and how human relationships (an essential ingredient in any startup) really work.

However, the downside to that is being too set in your ways. As we get older, it's easy to become inflexible and unable to see possibilities that are obvious to younger people. Surrounding herself with younger people, including entrepreneurs in their 20s and 30s, is one-way Lesonsky makes sure she has plenty of fresh perspectives.

Another advantage is a huge network of contacts. Most of 55 and older executives have spent decades in the work force and have hundreds of professional contacts to call on. That's not even counting your wide circle of family and friends. All of them can be sources of inspiration and help.

A huge disadvantage to older entrepreneurs is their outdated skill set. Let's face it. Sometimes, we don't learn to do things because we had no need to. Our secretaries can handle the "grunt work." That's why we should always refresh and update our skill set to, as they say, keep up with the times. Having an executive position before, you may not have had to do some tasks that come with being an entrepreneur. Being an entrepreneur will mean that you will have to get down to the nitty gritty, so better start learning!

Another advantage that Lesonsky points out is the financial resources old executives have that younger entrepreneurs might not have access to. Homes, collections, stocks and retirement accounts can all be called upon to fund your startup, since you will need to put some of your own skin in the game. However, reality is, you might need some of that money. With retirement closer than for 20-somethings, you have less room for error. Lesonsky advises not completely risking your nest egg. Instead, she suggests trying to bootstrap a low-cost business since there are tons of them to choose from.

The last positive note for starting late is basically being child-free. You're likely an empty nester with time on your hands. What better way to use it than by starting your own business?

113

There are more pros than cons to starting a business at a later age. Fear will not help you. Taking action does. Lesonsky has been a happy entrepreneur for more than six years now. If she can do it, why not you, too?

Chapter 15

Failure "Fail Big Today!"

Astro Teller talks about the unexpected benefit of failure during his Ted Talk. He states that success is built on failure. At Google X, they look for a huge problem that affects millions of people. They come up with a radical solution for the problem and in doing so, invent a breakthrough technology in solving the problem. As he said, "Great dreams are not just visions but they are visions that have concrete strategies in making it real".

In his company, failure is being celebrated. They celebrate each time they see holes in each breakthrough technology they come up with. They even promote teams made up of ten or more people just because they failed. How come? Why spend all that money, time and manpower for things they want to see fail? It is because every time they fail, they are provided with the opportunity to attack the problem in another way. They cross out multiple options by failing and end up with the biggest successes in their innovations. They approach the project by seeing it fail first before it can ultimately succeed, "Enthusiastic skepticism", as Teller puts it. Rather than see enthusiastic skepticism as the enemy, it is in fact the perfect companion to unbridled enthusiasm.

For example, the automated vertical farming they used to think was the solution for undernourishment was killed because staple crops like rice and grains cannot be grown this way. While the idea has merits, it wasn't feasible for staple crops and the company had to kill this project after exploring all the possible alternatives. Another project was a cargo ship that is lighter than air to ship food to landlocked countries to minimize expense and carbon footprints. The problem there is its production. Designing and building this type of cargo ship would cost the whopping amount of almost 200 million dollars. Google X is hellbent on finding the weak points of their ideas before investing on such expensive venture therefore ending up with termination of projects that had been proven to fail.

However, Teller says that seeing a flaw in their project doesn't always mean the end of it. Instead, they channel that setback into something productive. For instance, with the purpose of lessening car accidents happening all around the globe, they invented a car that can drive itself. Their first prototype was a Lexus Retrofitted Self-Driving car. These had been doing so well in the initial test run that they decide to give some to their employees to test them out for themselves. They discovered a major flaw in these cars. The car was originally made to do all the driving and give the controls back to the driver in case of emergency. What happened was that the drivers got complacent that they fail to take control of the car whenever it is needed therefore making it unsafe. The car was sent back to the drawing board when it had proven to be a failure. This failure allowed the creators to finetune this invention and they came up with a car where the "driver" is truly just a passenger. This new prototype has no steering wheel or even brakes. The only thing the driver has to do is get in the car, tell it where they want to go, and the car takes that person from point A to point B. This car is already being used in California and Texas, self-driving for over 1.4 million miles today.

Failure allowed these inventors to experience a shift in perspective. Having experienced a shift in paradigm, they are able to see multiple solutions that can greatly benefit mankind. Failure is encouraged because it is a progressive kind of failure. A shift in paradigm can prove to be much more helpful than being smart. Not being too set in your ways and being able to change as you go through failure will ultimately lead to success.

This is not about the old saying, 1% inspiration and 99% perspiration. That is saying you try and try until you succeed. If it didn't happen for you it is because you had not tried enough. That is not the case. Instead, whenever you fail, try differently. Whenever you fail, develop a mindset that does not see this as a setback but sees it as an opportunity for a bigger success. Do not attack a problem the same way over and over again. Learn about your mistakes and own up to it. Then once you are ready, you can face the problem differently and come up with better and more efficient solutions.

Businesses can fail. There is no going around that. Founders of startups such as Drawquest, Outbox and Prim had opened up with so much honestly as to why their businesses did not fly. While it can be safely assumed they are most probably drinking their deep personal losses away in the back of a bar, that is certainly not the case. Instead, they were honest and shared their failures to the public. Why? It is because they are hoping that people will learn from their mistakes and try to come up with different strategies in solving the problems that had stumped them.

In Silicon Valley, it's not necessarily frowned upon to create companies and then run them into the ground. In fact, many founders of failed companies find it easier to raise money for their second company. Investors know they are buying experience and the lessons learned from those failed endeavors.

In our family we have a saying "Get in the Game". Meaning get in the game, play hard, take risk, you will most certainly fail along the way but when you look back you will see how far you have come.

Chapter 16

Financial Considerations

Companies are downsizing, and middle managers are getting laid off. With senior level jobs disappearing left and right, workers are betting on the severance package to keep them afloat until they can find new jobs. However, much like the salary, severance pay can very much vary. The question that resurfaces today is, how much severance money should I be paid? Coupled with the embarrassment and frustration of losing a job, there is also the fear of losing one's income to factor in. It is, therefore, a momentary relief to receive a huge severance package.

The amount one can receive is dependent on so many factors: what type of employee are you (hourly or salaried), which management do you belong to (upper, middle or lower), what are the conditions of your dismissal and how long have you worked for the company. The employer will take these into consideration when creating offers. If you are part of upper management, your severance pay will undoubtedly be higher. Severance packages for upper management can range from 6 months of regular pay to a year or higher. The highest severance pay will be granted to tenured employees of more than 40 years and older than 60 years of age. Keep in mind that nothing is set in stone when it comes to severance pay. While your company can follow standard formulas in calculating how much money you are getting, that does not necessarily mean that the money they are offering is the same as the amount you are

119

entitled to. Companies would offer less but make it sweet enough for you to be tempted to accept immediately. Do not forget that you are losing your livelihood with no assurance of what's to come in the future. Instead of signing immediately, be sure to get a sound legal advice first. You should also always ask for more and request for extended healthcare benefits, job placement services, or gadgets like your company cell phone and laptop. Factor in unused vacation, sick time and unpaid overtime into negotiating your severance package.

The bottom line is you will find that working your way in up the company is just the same as working your way out of it. The employers are driven with their motivation to keep you happy upon exiting. This gives you more leverage for bargaining. Do your research for the reasonable benefits you can expect to get from your company and maximize them the best that you can. Losing a job is hard and finding another source of livelihood is even harder. To keep your head afloat for the meantime, a decent and fair severance pay would really go a long way.

After receiving your severance pay and saying goodbye to your desk of so many years, friends, colleagues and other people you may dislike, it is time to pick yourself up and go look for a job. Job hunt is daunting but the inevitable bills and expenses in looking for a job can be just as unnerving, too. The loss of income will hit you hard. What they never tell you is how looking for another source of income will further drain your savings.

What does it cost to look for a job?

To land a job, you must impress your potential employers by looking, sounding and acting professional and credible. That is perhaps the number one mandate in every corporate job hunt. With today's fast-paced society, managers and recruiters prefer scouring the internet to look for candidates. This is a much more convenient and faster way of looking for prospects. Therefore, these managers can expect anyone to be available at any time.

The most important thing you can allocate your money on is education. If you are having trouble looking for jobs that can fit your skill set, it is probably because your skills are outdated. Everyone needs an upgrade every now and then. Jobs look for necessary and specific skills and they won't adjust for the skills you already have. To impress potential employers, it is necessary to impress them with not only your personality but with your capabilities, also. Therefore, education becomes a must. You should always be able to learn new skills and hone your craft further. While education should be a right, it becomes a privilege with the exorbitant amount of money we spend on it. Additional training is commonly taught online and ranges from few hundred to a few thousand dollars, depending on the specialization. It is an expensive necessity.

Nowadays, applicants rely more on the Internet to look for jobs that are suited to their respective fields, capabilities and location. Technology is becoming cheaper, but it still costs a lot of money.

A common mistake among older executives looking for a job is sending out a dated resume. It is understandable since they haven't had the need to touch up on their resume for years but having a not-so-stellar resume to begin with will turn most employers off. Resume services offer writing professional resumes with all the relevant details in it. This includes packaging you in a way that will entice the employers to see you as someone they need to have in their company. Not only will this give you an edge over the steep competition for jobs, having your resume written by a professional will provide you an insight as to what the companies are currently looking for. The disadvantage is the cost. A writer can charge per hour or per job. Nevertheless, a complete and revised resume will cost from $100 to $500.

Career counseling provides you with an opportunity to have a professional look you over and coach you into the choosing right career path for you to take while teaching you the best possible ways of marketing yourself to companies. The way career counseling works is, they help you identify your strengths, provide you with strategies on how best to sell yourself and those strengths to employers, and establish a career path that aligns with your goals. It also can get very pricey. Many coaches charge $100 to $500 per hour. A couple of hours might not even be enough to have significant progress, nudging you to shell out more money.

The list of expenses can go on and on. The hard truth is, job search is not only frustrating, but it has proven to be also a very expensive ordeal. Job loss can cause the same amount of stress as that of experiencing a divorce. You will lose your income, but you are also forced to spend money during the job search, effectively draining your savings. Landing a job immediately isn't even a guarantee. Spending weeks and weeks without paycheck can be hard, making severance pay dwindle—especially when you are supporting your family and their needs.

So, how do you effectively manage your resources when looking for a job?

Having a stable job might have made you complacent. You haven't thought of how you spend your money for years now. Losing your job changes that. You must now begin to determine just how much you are spending and what goes to what. You must be aware of how much money goes into mortgage or rent, monthly payments, weekly grocery bill etc. Once you find out just how much money goes into these expenses, this allows you to have more foresight when it comes to spending. This will enable you to handle your savings with more care, and knowing which ventures and expenses are worth investing on.

Secondly, once you have determined your expenses, label them according to your needs. You must learn to prioritize and learn to cut back. Develop a budget plan that will eliminate the fatty expenses you can live without. Be frugal and don't go reckless with your savings by having unnecessary purchases. You never know just how long you have to hold out until you can land a job.

Lastly, get a part-time job. While looking for a full-time job, having a part-time job to pay the bills will not only help ease some of the financial burden but it can help you stay afloat for a longer period. Go on websites that offer part-time jobs that allow you to work from home. Having a part-time job will help you broaden your horizon and widen your skill set.

While severance pay can really be a big help, everything will eventually be up to you once you start looking for jobs and managing your finances in the process. It always pays to be wiser financially in this tough economy.

It is estimated that the cost of looking for a job combined with the loss of income can range between $4,000 to $6,000 per month. With executives being out of work on average 57 week, this amount can total $57,000 to $86,000. As one can imagine, this can take a toll on retirement savings.

Chapter 17

Career Coaches

It's a tough job market out there, especially for older executives. The competition in the job market had become steeper with tech savvy, younger candidates, vying for the same positions who will work more for lesser pay.

Some people employ the help of career coaches to land new jobs. However, reinforcing career coaches' help can often get pricey. What are career coaches and what do they do that some people find it necessary to invest their money on them?

According to the most basic and simple definition, a career coach is someone who assesses you, identifies the right niche for you and helps you transition into that new role. In an interview with LearnVest, Donna Sweidan, a career coach of 15 years, she states that approaches her job as a "discipline comprised of two similar but distinct tracks: coaching and counseling. The goal is to support people in making informed decisions about their career development and trajectory, as well as offering various tools that they can use—résumés, cover letters, LinkedIn profiles—to meet those goals."

Coming from an objective point of view, coaches will assess your current skills, experience and strengths. From then on career coaches explore potential career options that are best suited for you and make a clear, realistic action steps to help you achieve your goals. He or she will help you transition through it by guiding you through the current demands of employers, changes in the work environment and of course, personal development.

Sweidan identifies two major components in career coaching. "Coaching" involves helping the clients take concrete steps to achieve their career goals and objectives while "Counseling" is more on the process, meaning a coach must focus more on the behavioral, emotional or psychological issues that could hamper the person's drive to succeed. "But the core value of career coaching is to help people assess their professional situations with a greater degree of honesty, curiosity, empathy and compassion," Sweidan added.

For Sweidan, the most common misconceptions about hiring a career coach are that effective job search will eventually boil down to a well-done resume and that the coaches are the ones responsible for finding you a job. That isn't all that there is to it.

A person, Sweidan said, can expect "career confidence, insight, encouragement and inspiration" when working with a career coach. If you think that a career coach is for you, you must be prepared to spend at least $100 to $500 per hour. Furthermore, to see a significant progress, people have to spend up to 20 hours with their coaches on average. Before you go committing yourself to a career coach and spending a large sum of money, it is most important to know about the pros and cons of hiring one and avoid spending huge, unnecessary amount of money.

Let us start with the cons.

The first thing you should watch out for are the frauds. There are always going to be "coaches" claiming to help you land your dream jobs with high success rates when, in fact, they do not have the necessary background and experience to support those claims.

There is also buyer's remorse. After committing yourself to a coach, you may end up feeling regret for availing their services due to a lot of possible reasons. Some people might engage the career coach for the wrong motives—this just might not be what they need. Another reason is that you don't get along with your coach. Finding the right coach for yourself can truly present a challenge. Some coaches can be so imposing and rather than listen to you, they end up shoving their biases, own agendas and opinions down your throat. Sometimes, with the wrong coach, you might find them thinking that they know better than you.

Lastly, the greatest and most obvious con in hiring a coach is the cost. There is a strategy employed by some coaches that they charge an unjustifiable amount of money as a way to market themselves to convince you that their services are better. This plays with the myth that the more expensive a product is, the better and more prestigious it is.

Also, being unemployed, hiring a coach can put a huge dent in your savings. It is, therefore, important to know and make sure which expenses are the most necessary to invest in.

Now, let's move on with the pros.

The main advantage of hiring a coach is the motivation. A coach will not only push you to find the right job with their tools and superb knowledge in the job market, but the thought of spending a lot of money on something will motivate you to actually follow things through. Also, when facing discouragement and rejection, your coach will be there to help you pick yourself up and get you back on the right track. Your spirit will become more motivated and hopeful.

Technically, they are an expert in knowing just what the employers look for in their employees. With this knowledge, they can provide you with a better understanding of properly presenting yourself on your resume, cover letter and job interviews that will help you fit in with the organization, culture of the company and impress your prospective bosses.

As mentioned earlier, a huge portion of a career coach's job is to identify your strengths and weaknesses. By having these identified, you will gain insight into the combination of skills and abilities that you (and no one else) can bring to the table. Knowing your worth as a professional will help you tremendously during the job searching process and knowing which path to take. This will boost your confidence and narrow down the paths you take. It is almost analogous to firing a gun and hitting the target precisely compared to throwing a bunch of rocks and hoping one of them can hit the target.

Many people choose their careers based on the salary, only to discover unhappiness and dissatisfaction on the other end of the spectrum. Career coaches are trained to get to know you, your personality, qualifications, and passions, then help you to find a career that is challenging, promising, and fulfilling.

These are pros and cons of hiring a career coach that must be taken into consideration to gauge if you have the need and the means for a coach. It is always important to weigh out the positive and the negative points before taking the leap and committing one's self—especially with huge investments such as this one.

Chapter 18

Stories

Javier had always trusted himself. He knew that he would one day have his own business as long as he worked hard and persevered. He first worked as a 7-Eleven store manager and he thoroughly enjoyed being one. He loved being at the store, interacting with customers and leading his own little crew to work with. He had always been entrepreneurial, never once losing sight of his dream of becoming his own boss. While still conservative with his money, he saved and reinvested in a few steadily growing real estate holdings in the booming market of Austin, Texas.

Eventually, he had saved up enough money to buy a franchisee. With no second thought, Javier chose 7-Eleven. "To be honest, I did not look at other franchises," he shared. "Owning a franchise, you have a lot of support and you're owning a 7-Eleven franchise, so they already laid the groundwork for you." He prepared for his store like any franchisee would. He gathered enough capital and used it wisely. Javier was even more excited when he found out about the Store Manager Franchisee Assistance Program. This program enabled him to be a candidate for special benefits such as financial support, incentivizing corporate benefits, and other items since he had a strong background in making corporate stores profitable.

He only had one thought after that, "Awesome!"

Opening his very first store came with a fresh set of concern and fears. While franchisees essentially run a small business, a store can still come with its own challenges and obstacles. Franchisees can overcome these by overseeing store operations, leading employees and managing inventory with skill and efficiency. While this could be scary, Javier was assured that he will not be facing all these alone. Through trusted Franchise Sales Representatives, Javier can tap into the knowledge of over 3,500 corporate employees tirelessly working to give him the advantage that he needs.

"I've only been at this store for a short while, but I learned a lot of the customers' names, and when they walk in I'm able to interact with them on a personal level. I always ask them, 'You want the usual?' and chitchat about personal stuff. It makes them feel like a part of the store, where people know your name," Javier says.

Javier, being a motorcycle enthusiast, likes a fast and fun life but he still manages to stay focused. Riding a motorbike requires constant attention to your surroundings and he stressed that at 7-Eleven, great training is the foundation for pin-point focus on the job ahead. The training program combines classroom and in-store training on store operations, merchandising and procedures, financial information and employee relations. The team you build can be one of the keys in making the business prosper and Javier stressed they are as important to him as the community he serves. "I create a culture of caring with my employees. I build a team that's flexible, so they can cover each other in times of need. It's a good approach. It makes them have a personal attachment to you. It's worked for me. Once I do build a team, they stay with me quite a long time."

Javier's dream of becoming a business owner has become a reality. He became a servant leader within the community he serves while being a great representative of the 7-Eleven brand.

According to Javier, to be a successful franchisee, one must be a people's person. "You've really got to back up the quality you sell in your store with a place where people want to come. Build a relationship with the neighborhood that your store is in and then allow your employees to be themselves, because when they feel comfortable, they smile. Take pride in what you're selling."

Another inspiring franchisee success story is that of Fields and his wife, Shvonna. The couple have three kids under the age of ten. As parents, they knew just how expensive buying sports equipment can be when a child wants to play hockey, baseball or any other sport they fancy. Of course, they couldn't very well deprive their kids especially if they decide not just to stick to one sport but to try out several of them.

Fields is a co-owner of Play It Again Sports with Jake Pinger in North Spokane WA. The sports franchise is something very familiar to

Fields already. When he attended college, he worked at a Play It Again Sports store in Spokane under another owner. After that, he moved on to become a manager at a Spokane restaurant. But being a manager had neither fulfilled nor made him happy. He missed working in the retail sports shop.

Fields had observed throughout his career in sports retail how big the financial impact of kids playing sports can be. Kids grow fast which means they can easily outgrow sports equipment and he knows that they do not come cheap. Kids can also just lose interest in the sport or activity they swore up and down they would love after getting all the equipment necessary for it. Fields was more than inspired by his love for sports retail and his parental insight on kids who are active in sports.

His store was about 4,000-square-feet of retail space in front and 2,500-square-feet in the back area and carries about half-new and half-used gear. "We have equipment for just about any sport being played in the Spokane area, including basketball, baseball, golf and disc golf, lacrosse, skiing, skating, biking and more," he said. Various kinds of equipment are also available at his store, including big items like treadmills, elliptical trainers and exercise bikes, as well as smaller items like weights, Kettle bells and boxing gloves. Fields, who also coaches both baseball and hockey in the community, said he also provides information about Spokane sports leagues and organization on the store's website, as well as supplies for coaches.

"I think the store is a good thing for the community. It gives more kids a chance to play sports that they may not have had a chance because of the cost," Fields said. In his store, customers can either trade in equipment or take credit or cash for sports gear they can no longer use. Fields said that the pricing on the gear will depend on the brand, the quality and the shape the item is in. The biggest selling sports gear right now in the store is hockey, baseball and soccer equipment, he said.

Play It Again Sports has a full-service repair shop for bikes and other sports equipment at the back of the store, as well as skate sharpening, snowboard and ski tune-ups, and lacrosse head stringing. Skiing packages, including boots and skis, or snowboard rentals are also offered at the shop.

"I'm excited to be part of something in the community where people can come in, and trade in sports equipment," Fields said. "I think it is giving more kids a chance to play".

Combining his own resources and his passion to start his own business in the field he loves the most which is sports retail, Fields is able to fulfill his dreams while giving back to the community. He gets satisfaction knowing that he is doing his part by helping kids get into sports and become more active. Driven by his love for his own kids, he is able to help others with his business.

Business ownership promises a level of autonomy and fulfillment that can't be given by being a mere employee. Business ownership also provides big opportunities of giving back to the community that had nourished and helped you to become who you are right now. This will ultimately lead your life from pursuit of success to that of significance. Don't we want to leave a lasting legacy on this earth? "I am too old to own my own business "should never become an excuse to stay I your comfort zone.

It is fact that 25% of baby boomers hoped to start a business or nonprofit within 5 to 10 years, according to a survey conducted by the MetLife Foundation. Here are some of the old entrepreneurs who braved the unknown and found greater rewards than working for someone had given them all these years.

From Springdale, Ark, 65-year-old Jim Butenschoen was fed up with the corporate world after spending more than 20 years in the IT industry. He had always nourished a desire to go into business himself. After finding the courage to do so, he opened the Career Academy of Hair Design starting with 6 employees at first. Many years later, he now has 32 employees working at his 4 growing establishments. "Despite all the ups and downs, I have never done anything more satisfying," he says. "I wake up so satisfied and secure. Every day has more challenges and hurdles, but they're my challenges and hurdles." Though some people his age retire, he says, "I don't want to stop working because I'm having so much fun."

Rand Smith also had the same inclinations as Jim. Rand had worked in the optical industry for over 30 years. He decided to go into business on his own and he shared that journey with the person he trusts the most, his wife, Janeel. The Smiths, both in their 50s, tapped into their retirement funds and opened EyeSmith Sport & Fashion Optical, which is a high-end optical store in Kansas City that sells prescription fashion and sport performance eyewear. Janeel said that her husband became very tired of "corporate bologna." They had so much more fun getting up every day and going to work now because they can determine what is important. "And that is our clients," she added.

Carol Gardner had a different motivation from the rest when starting her own business. She was 52, newly divorced, broke and depressed. She was going through so much in that period of her life. You would think that starting a business on top of other tragedies she was facing might just be the last thing on her mind. But it is as if Carol was fated to run her own business. Having a business might just be what helped her get through all of the tragedies in her life.

It was winning a local Christmas card contest with a picture of a dog and a funny quip that had given Carol a stroke of inspiration. She had just gotten a dog as recommended by her therapist. The card made Carol think of starting a greeting card company which she named after her dog, Zelda. In 2010, Zelda Wisdom was valued at roughly $50 million. It goes to show that whenever crisis happens, sometimes they can provide you with ways of achieving your dreams.

Starting and running a business isn't going to be easy. There will be challenges at every turn. It will take an enormous amount of sacrifices, hard work and discipline to reach success. As a result, it shouldn't come as a surprise that the older and much wiser part of the population might even be better at venturing into entrepreneurship. So, don't count yourself out just yet, no matter what your age is. Success can most definitely come to anyone at any time.

Pete was 56 years old, had worked in the trades as an electrician for 25 years. Throughout his career he did well in investing in the stock market and lived conservatively. This paid off when Pete lost his job, he was able to take the time he needed to look at his options. Pete had a growth mindset and was determined to investigate what opportunities were available to him.

Pete attended a Franchise Expo in his home town and came across a consulting company who specialized in the franchise industry and guiding their clients in evaluating what franchises might be a good fit. Pete spent time with the consultant mapping out his next chapter in life by asking the easy and the hard questions. Questions came up regarding risk, financial wherewithal, leadership and sales skills, stage of life goals, his passions, where he would like to live, industries he saw himself working in, and more.

As Pete progressed down this road, he found that there were key things that were of great importance to him and that he wanted to make sure he would achieve going forward. He also took an honest look at his quality of life and what that meant to him now, when he would see himself ready for retirement, his purpose and what would get him up in the morning. He looked at other ideas such as starting his own business or buying an existing one. After weighing his options, he felt that the franchise model best suited him at this time.

From there the consultant was able to take the information Pete provided and filtered through hundreds of franchises to find ones that had a proven track record of matching the goals Pete set out for himself. In the end, Pete chose to purchase a home inspection business. The financial investment was within his budget, the quality of life components gave him the freedom he was looking for and the brand was well established and had strong validation.

There were fears that popped up along the way, yet Pete was diligent in asking the right questions to work his way through the uncertainties.

Pete is now a proud owner, plans on working hard as he has done in the past, yet in the end of the day he sits down and knows that all he had done was to help build his own business not someone else's and he was on his way to secure his future.

Sheila worked in the banking industry for 20 years. She developed strong leadership and management skills along with her trade. When Sheila had children, she and her husband decided it was best for Sheila to stay home and be with her children. Years later when her children were grown, Sheila decided it was time to go back in the market and continue her career. However, this time she began to think about owning her own business. She wanted something that would be in the child education field. She also wanted to have flexibility in her schedule to still spend key moments with her own children. Lastly with her banking background she was focused on a healthy return on her investment.

Sheila enlisted the services of a franchise consultant. Together they developed a detailed business model that would be used to filter through the multitude of franchise options. It took Sheila close to a year to find the right opportunity as she was very risk adverse and wanted to be very comfortable with her decision. Sheila bought a children's tutoring franchise and now able to build her business in a way that mirrors her family's goals and objectives.

Patti came from the IT industry where she owned a successful consulting firm. She was an entrepreneur at heart. She knew what it takes to start a business up on her own and what it takes to build it into a successful venture. Patti also knew she wanted to expand her business holdings and diversify her investments. She also was looking for a recurring income to offset the ebbs and flows of the consulting industry.

She had her sites on growing a portfolio of businesses over time and therefore needed a business that was scalable. Since she had already owned a business, she wanted to look at franchises as she knew speed to market and buying a proven system was the best investment decision for her both as it relates to her financially but also for investment of time. Patti had a passion for children and building into their future. She found a perfect franchise that teach children the art of cooking. This was not only going to be a good business investment but also one that was going to be fun. Patti can now say she is on her way to building her empire.

Steve was 45 and worked in the broadcasting business. He got word from senior management that later that year he would be losing his job due to a corporate restructuring. Steve didn't waste searching for viable options. Such as looking for other employment, starting his own business, buying an existing company or buying a franchise. He knew he was too young to retire, was frustrated with the lack of loyalty found in corporate America and uncertainty in the job market. This was not his first time being faced with the effects of corporate downsizing.

This time he wanted to control his own destiny.

Steve started his search on his own and eventually determined it was better for him to seek help from a professional consultant. Together they looked at industries where he could capitalize on his past skills and experiences. He had a passion for helping people with finding the right job as he himself found the journey to be one that of frustration. He also studied the employer side of the market and quickly found that every employer was wrestling with finding qualified staff. Steve took time pondering this and determined that he was either going to run from the problem or become part of the solution. Steve chose the latter. He felt he would be offering a great service to both the employers as well as those seeking meaningful employment.

Steve ended up buying a staff agency franchise. Not just any staffing agency but he hooked his wagon to the world's largest one. He was able to secure a great territory and loved the support that corporate was offering him to help him succeed. Steve is now in control of his destiny as he set out to achieve for himself.

Joe and his fiancé Suzanne were to be married in the summer. Joe was a partner in a printing company and Suzanne owned a boutique woman's clothing store. They both were concerned about the future of their business as competition from the internet was eating away at the profits and created big swings in the market.

Being entrepreneurs, they knew their goal was to open up business they both could run together. They wanted a recession resistant industry, a recurring revenue, something that was scalable to continue to build wealth. Yet with both of them in their later 50's, speed to market was critical. They had been down the path of business ownership and knew the franchise model was the best choice for them. They also knew they needed to secure the help of a professional to navigate this journey. They were very busy with their existing companies as well as planning a wedding, so their time was a commodity and wanted a franchise expert on their team.

Immediately the team began look in various industries. They went from food, to massage to sports, to senior care never anticipating they were going to land where they did. They found a dry-cleaning business and upon studying the dry-cleaning industry together with the opportunity to be part of the world's largest dry-cleaning company, they knew this was the perfect fit. The potential revenue was staggering, fully scalable, recession resistant and a semi absent model. The best part is they were able to combine the ability to buy and existing up and running business and get all the benefits of a franchise. This meant immediate cash flow, and increased market share. They liked it so much they bought three of them.

Chapter 19

Conclusion:

Thank you for reading my book. I hope it was helpful to lay out in front of you the multiple steps one goes through when in a career transition and are trying to decide for yourself "What is my Next Move".

As much as I would like to lead you to the conclusion and tell you what your next move is, unfortunately only you can answer that for yourself for you know what is best for you and your family.

It is important that you sincerely evaluate each of the 5 stages of a career transition

1. Retirement

2. Work for Corporate America

3. Start up a new company

4. Buy an existing company

5. Buy a franchise

Like a scientist, do your homework and let the facts lead you to your decision. In the end you will need a little faith and the ability to trust and invest in yourself.

Appendix 1

Resources

ABC Franchise. (2014, March 27). Success rate of a new franchise business vs an independent start up. Retrieved from Franchisewithalwaysbestcare.com: https://franchisewithalwaysbestcare.com/success-rate-of-a-new-franchise-business-vs-an-independent-start-up/

Allis, R. (n.d.). The history of entrepreneurship. Retrieved from The Startup Guide: http://startupguide.com/world/the-history-of-entrepreneurship/

Anicich, E. M., & Hirsch, J. B. (2017, March 22). Why being a middle manager is so exhausting? Retrieved from Harvard Business Review: https://hbr.org/2017/03/why-being-a-middle-manager-is-so-exhausting

Backman, M. (2016, September 16). Is 70 the new retirement age? Retrieved from USAToday.com: https://www.usatoday.com/story/money/personalfinance/2016/09/16/is-70-the-new-retirement-age/90256526/

Bergelann, H., Moen, E. R., Roed, K., & Skogstrom, J. F. (2009). Entepreneurship: Origins and returns. R&D, Industry Dynamics and Public Policy.

Beri, S. (2015, May 4). How do you manage job search frustration? Retrieved from fortune.com: http://fortune.com/2015/05/04/how-do-you-manage-job-search-frustration/

Bernard. (2016, November 10). 25 successful entrepreneurs who quit their jobs to pursue their passions. Retrieved from Invoice Berry Blog: http://blog.invoiceberry.com/2016/11/25-successful-entrepreneurs-quit-jobs-passions/

Bookshelves, Notes, Self-Awareness. (2012, January). Mindset by Carol Dweck: A summary. Retrieved from Alexvermeer.com: https://alexvermeer.com/why-your-mindset-important/

Bort, J. (2016, October 24). 9 tech trends that will make billions of dollars starting in 2017. Retrieved from Business Insider: http://www.businessinsider.com/9-tech-trends-2017-billions-2016-10/#ai-and-advanced-machine-learning-1

Brennfleck, K., & Brennfleck, K. M. (n.d.). When you're looking for a calling, not just a job. Retrieved from http://www.christiancareercenter.com/advice-and-resources/career-and-calling-articles/looking-for-a-calling-not-just-a-job

Bruder, J. (n.d.). The psychological price og entrepreneurship. Retrieved from Inc.com: https://www.inc.com/magazine/201309/jessica-bruder/psychological-price-of-entrepreneurship.html

Buford, B. (2008). Halftime: Moving from success to significance. Zondervan.

Buy an existing business or franchise. (n.d.). Retrieved from SBA.gov: https://www.sba.gov/business-guide/plan/buy-existing-business-franchise

Canty, A. (2012, October 1). Entrepreneur self-assessment: 9 professional tools and tests. Retrieved from Grasshopper.com: http://grasshopper.com/blog/9-professional-assessment-tools/

Career Alley. (2016, September 9). Should you get a career coach--pros and cons. Retrieved from Careeralley.com: https://careeralley.com/career-coaches-pros-and-cons/

Chay, D. (2009, September 14). A synopsis of Bob Buford's book "HALFTIME". Retrieved from davidchayblogspot.com: http://davidchay.blogspot.com/2009/09/synopsis-of-bob-bulfords-book-halftime.html

Cheeks, D. (2013, July 9). 10 things you should know about career coaching. Retrieved from Forbes.com: https://www.forbes.com/sites/learnvest/2013/07/09/10-things-you-should-know-about-career-coaching/#420347967d5e

Clay, K. (n.d.). When things go wrong, should you quit or wait to get fired. Retrieved from Fastcompany.com: https://www.fastcompany.com/3052937/when-things-go-wrong-should-you-quit-or-wait-to-get-fired

Connick, W. (2017, April 27). The average cost of retirement is $738,400: Will you have enough? Retrieved from USAToday.com: https://www.usatoday.com/story/money/personalfinance/retirement/2017/04/27/the-average-cost-of-retirement-is-738400-will-you-have-enough/100738100/

Daszkowski, D. (2016, October 26). The pros and cons of buying an existing franchise. Retrieved from thebalance.com: https://www.thebalance.com/the-pros-and-cons-of-buying-an-existing-franchise-1350090

Daugherty, G. (2017, May 1). The pros and (mostly) cons of early retirement. Retrieved from Investopedia.com:

http://www.investopedia.com/articles/personal-finance/073114/pros-and-mostly-cons-early-retirement.asp

DeMers, J. (2014, December 1). 5 fears you'll need to conquer before starting a business. Retrieved from Entrepreneur.com: https://www.entrepreneur.com/article/240275

Dvorsky, G. (2017, March 28). Robots are already replacing human workers at an alarming rate. Retrieved from Gizmodo: http://gizmodo.com/robots-are-already-replacing-human-workers-at-an-alarmi-1793718198

Dweck, C. S. (2006). Mindset: The new psychology of success. New York: Random House, Inc.

Ennico, C. (2008, June 18). Before you buy that small business. Retrieved from Entrepreneur.com: https://www.entrepreneur.com/article/195020

Evanston, A. (n.d.). Do you have the entrepreneurial mindset? Retrieved from Excelle.monster.com: http://excelle.monster.com/benefits/articles/3091-do-you-have-the-entrepreneurial-mindset

Fast Company Staff. (2005, November 21). Celebrate Failure. Retrieved from Fastcompany.com: https://www.fastcompany.com/918958/celebrate-failure

Fisher, A. (2015, January 15). When to quit your job and start your own business. Retrieved from Fortune.com: http://fortune.com/2015/01/15/starting-business-entrepreneur/

Franchises vs. Startups, What Makes More Sense for You? (n.d.). Retrieved from Franchisehelp.com:

https://www.franchisehelp.com/franchisee-resource-center/franchises-vs-startups-what-makes-more-sense-for-you/

Frankle, N. (n.d.). Buying an existing business: 7 steps to success. Retrieved from Wealthpilgrim.com: http://wealthpilgrim.com/buying-an-existing-business-7-steps-to-success/

Garfinkle, J. (n.d.). Difference between male and female leadership. Retrieved from Careeradvancementblog.com: https://careeradvancementblog.com/male-female-leadership

Garver, L. (2014, 24 September). Overcoming executive job search challenges: Baby boomers. Retrieved from Careerdirectionsllc.com: https://careerdirectionsllc.com/overcome-executive-job-search-challenges-baby-boomers/

Gates, B. (2015, December 7). What you believe affects what you achieve. Retrieved from Gatesnotes.com: https://www.gatesnotes.com/Books/Mindset-The-New-Psychology-of-Success

Gerber, M. E. (n.d.). 4 personality traits all entrepreneurs must have. Retrieved from Inc.com: https://www.inc.com/michael-gerber/4-personality-traits-all-entrepreneurs-must-have.html

Gibson, J. (2014, March 19). Celebrating failure: How to make a hit out of misses. Retrieved from Entrepreneur.com: https://www.entrepreneur.com/article/232323

Gillet, R., & Feloni, R. (2016, April 16). 19 highly successful people who prove it's never too late to change careers. Retrieved from Business Insider: http://www.businessinsider.com/successful-people-who-made-a-big-career-change-2016-4/#martha-stewart-was-a-full-time-model-until-as-a-25-year-old-mother-she-found-few-modeling-jobs-coming-her-way-after-a-stint-as-a-wall-street-stockbroker-stewart-turned-h

Gordon, J. S. (2014, February). Entrepreneurship in American History. Imprimis.

Hannon, K. (2013, October 23). The 11 biggest mistakes older job hunters make. Retrieved from Forbes.com: https://www.forbes.com/sites/kerryhannon/2013/10/23/the-11-biggest-mistakes-older-job-hunters-make/#387967f79cd1

History of American Entrepreneurship. (2012, August 31). Retrieved from Ground Report: http://www.groundreport.com/history-of-american-entrepreneurship/

Hopler, W. (2011, August 2). How to find hope in any situation. Retrieved from Crosswalk.com: http://www.crosswalk.com/faith/spiritual-life/how-to-find-hope-in-any-situation-11636168.html

How to buy a business. (n.d.). Retrieved from Entrepreneur.com: https://www.entrepreneur.com/article/79638

How working with a career coach can help. (n.d.). Retrieved from Personalcareermanagement.com: https://www.personalcareermanagement.com/individual-services/career-coaching/

Hsu, T. (2009, April 10). Job market is especially cruel for older workers. Retrieved from LATimes.com: http://articles.latimes.com/2009/apr/10/business/fi-grayjobs10

Interview with Fabian Martinez: Director of Franchise Sales for Honest-1 Auto Care. (n.d.). Retrieved from Franchisedirect.com:

http://www.franchisedirect.com/successstories/honest-1-auto-care/12510/4116/

Interview with George Petrides: Founder of Wild Bird Centers of America. (n.d.). Retrieved from Franchisedirect.com: http://www.franchisedirect.com/successstories/wild-bird-centers-of-america/14059/4114/

Interview with Matt Kurowski: Vice President of Marketing and Franchise Development for Soccer Shots. (n.d.). Retrieved from Franchisedirect.com: http://www.franchisedirect.com/successstories/soccer-shots/13318/4115/

JD. (n.d.). 10 Big Ideas from Mindset: The New Psychology of Success. Retrieved from Sources of Insight: http://sourcesofinsight.com/10-big-ideas-from-mindset-the-new-psychology-of-success/

Job searching? Tried everything and frustrated? (n.d.). Retrieved from monster.ca: https://www.monster.ca/career-advice/article/job-searching-tried-everything-canada

Judy, J. (n.d.). Franchise or startup? You decide. Retrieved from Entrepreneur.com: https://www.entrepreneur.com/article/251728

Kritikos, A. S. (n.d.). Entrepreneurs and their impact on jobs and economic growth. Retrieved from IZA World of Labor: https://wol.iza.org/articles/entrepreneurs-and-their-impact-on-jobs-and-economic-growth/long

Laskow, S. (2014, October 24). How retirement was invented. Retrieved from TheAtlantic.com: https://www.theatlantic.com/business/archive/2014/10/how-retirement-was-invented/381802/

Lesonsky, R. (2014, June 24). The pros and cons of starting a business over 55. Retrieved from Score.org: https://www.score.org/blog/pros-and-cons-starting-business-over-55

Loving to serve the community. (2017, February 27). Retrieved from Franchiseresales.com: http://www.franchiseresales.com/index.cfm?action=successStories

Mamlet, R. (2017, 21 February). Gender in the job interview. Retrieved from Chronicle.com: http://www.chronicle.com/article/Gender-in-the-Job-Interview/239258

McNeal, M. (n.d.). Rise of the machines: the future has lots of robots, few jobs for humans. Retrieved from Wired.com: https://www.wired.com/brandlab/2015/04/rise-machines-future-lots-robots-jobs-humans/

Miceli, M. (2015, September 17). Google tops reputation rankings for corporate responsibility. Retrieved from USNEWS.com: https://www.usnews.com/news/articles/2015/09/17/google-tops-reputation-rankings-for-corporate-responsibility

Microsoft Corporate Responsibility. (n.d.). Retrieved from Microsoft.com: https://www.microsoft.com/en-us/about/corporate-responsibility

Mohr, T. S. (2014, 25 August). Why women won't apply for jobs unless they're 100% qualified. Retrieved from Harvard Business Review: https://hbr.org/2014/08/why-women-dont-apply-for-jobs-unless-theyre-100-qualified

Myers, F. R. (n.d.). 10 challenges senior executives face in the job search. Retrieved from careerpotential.com: https://careerpotential.com/career-advice-article/10-challenges-senior-executives-face-job-search/

Pant, P. (2016, November 30). But I don't want to retire. Retrieved from The Balance: https://www.thebalance.com/but-i-dont-want-to-retire-453987

Patel, S. (2015, January 5). Success can come at any age. Just look at these 6 successful entrepreneurs. Retrieved from Entrepreneur.com: https://www.entrepreneur.com/article/241346

Patterson, T.-E. (2014, December 9). 10 fears you must overcome when starting a business. Retrieved from Entrepreneur.com: https://www.entrepreneur.com/article/240592

Petroff, A. (2017, March 24). U.S. workers face higher risk of being replaced by robots. Here's why. Retrieved from CNN.com: http://money.cnn.com/2017/03/24/technology/robots-jobs-us-workers-uk/index.html

Price, R. W. (2011, April 21). What's the evolution of entrepreneurship in America? Retrieved from Global Entrepreneurship Institute: https://news.gcase.org/2011/04/21/whats-the-evolution-of-entrepreneurship-in-america/

Pros and cons of being an entrepreneur. (n.d.). Retrieved from Southuniversity.edu: http://source.southuniversity.edu/pros-and-cons-of-being-an-entrepreneur-96101.aspx

Riggs, J. (2004, October 28). Restaurant success stories. Retrieved from Entrepreneur.com: https://www.entrepreneur.com/article/73390

Robinson, J. (2013, January 12). What are the pros and cons of hiring a career coach and what are the important characteristics to consider before hiring one? Retrieved from Quora.com: https://www.quora.com/What-are-the-pros-and-cons-of-hiring-a-career-coach-and-what-are-the-important-characteristics-to-consider-before-hiring-one

Rojanasakul, M. (2017, May 8). More robots, fewer jobs. Retrieved from Bloomberg: https://www.bloomberg.com/graphics/2017-more-robots-fewer-jobs/

Schappel, C. (2015, May 1). 4 major differences between male and female job candidates. Retrieved from hrmorning.com: http://www.hrmorning.com/4-major-differences-between-male-and-female-job-candidates/

Secrets of becoming a successful master franchisee. (2017, February 7). Retrieved from Globalfranchisemagazine.com: http://www.globalfranchisemagazine.com/advice/secrets-of-becoming-a-successful-master-franchisee

Shane, S. (2013, May 7). The pros and cons of franchising your business. Retrieved from Entrepreneur.com: https://www.entrepreneur.com/article/226489

Sherman, E. (n.d.). 10 reasons why now is the best time to start your own business. Retrieved from Inc.com: https://www.inc.com/erik-sherman/10-reasons-why-now-is-the-best-time-to-start-your-business.html

Straits, D. (2009, January 5). Emotional stages of a job loss. Retrieved from theladders.com: https://www.theladders.com/p/1897/emotional-stages-job-loss

Surprising facts about gender in the job search. (n.d.). Retrieved from the undercoverrecruiter.com: http://theundercoverrecruiter.com/do-men-and-women-approach-the-job-hunt-differently/

Symonds, M. (2015, January 15). 7questions to find out if you're ready to be an entrepreneur in 2015. Retrieved from Forbes.com: https://www.forbes.com/sites/mattsymonds/2015/01/15/how-to-know-if-youre-ready-to-be-an-entrepreneur-in-2015/#5c26d246692a

Tahmincioglu, E. (2008, August 25). Layoffs move up ladder to middle management. Retrieved from NBCNEWS.com: http://www.nbcnews.com/id/26292996/ns/business-careers/t/layoffs-move-ladder-middle-management/#.WVxhSRXytH0

Teller, A. (2016, May 9). The unexpected benefit of celebrating failure [Video File]. Retrieved from https://www.youtube.com/watch?v=2t13Rq4oc7A&t=89s

Templeman, M. (2014, June 20). 20 reasons to start your own business. Retrieved from Entrepreneur.com: https://www.entrepreneur.com/article/234916

The National Academies of Sciences, E. a. (2007). In Rising above the gathering storm: Energizing and employing America for a brighter economic future (pp. 68-106). Washington, D.C.: The National Academies Press.

The role of faith in spiritual growth. (n.d.). Retrieved from cru.org: https://www.cru.org/train-and-grow/spiritual-growth/beginning-with-god/the-role-of-faith-in-spiritual-growth.html

The Toms Story. (n.d.). Retrieved from Toms.com: http://www.toms.com/corporate-responsibility

The Walt Disney Company: A leader in corporate social responsibility. (2013, June 10). Retrieved from Businessreviewusa.com: http://www.businessreviewusa.com/leadership/3827/The-Walt-Disney-Company-A-Leader-In-Corporate-Social-Responsibility

Trapp, R. (2014, March 31). Successful leaders celebrate their failures. Retrieved from Forbes.com: https://www.forbes.com/sites/rogertrapp/2014/03/31/successful-leaders-celebrate-their-failures/#10b656f26d14

Updegrave, W. (2017, April 17). What to do when you want to retire but don't have enough money. Retrieved from Time.com: http://time.com/money/4732364/retirement-advice-late-career-low-savings/

Vernon, S. (2017, April 5). Why 70 is the new 65 for retirement. Retrieved from CBSNEWS.com: https://www.cbsnews.com/news/why-70-is-the-new-65-for-retirement/

Warren, R. (2002). The Purpose Driven Life. Zondervan.

Wayman, M. (2014, July 9). Your career at 50: Challenges of the middle-aged career search. Retrieved from Huffingtonpost.com: http://www.huffingtonpost.com/mark-wayman/your-career-at-50-challen_b_5294727.html

Weinreb, E. (2011, September 15). When age and gender work against your job search. Retrieved from Forbes.com: https://www.forbes.com/sites/work-in-progress/2011/09/15/when-age-and-gender-work-against-your-job-search/#4fb8c2663156

What does a career coach do? (n.d.). Retrieved from careers.socialworkers.org: http://careers.socialworkers.org/findajob/articles/coach.asp

What is career coaching? (n.d.). Retrieved from Wolfgangcareercoaching.com: https://www.wolfgangcareercoaching.com/career-tools/what-is-career-coaching/

Wilding, M. (n.d.). 7 steps to surviving job loss. Retrieved from psychcentral.com: https://psychcentral.com/blog/archives/2014/02/11/7-steps-to-surviving-job-loss/

Williams, M. (n.d.). What are the pros and cons of hiring a career coach. Retrieved from Noomii.com: http://career.noomii.com/pros-cons-hiring-career-coach/

Wong, K. (2015, August 20). The five stages of grief after losing a job. Retrieved from lifehacker.com: http://lifehacker.com/the-five-stages-of-grief-after-losing-a-job-1725201444

Zahorsky, D. (2016, August 9). Pros and cons of buying a franchise. Retrieved from thebalance.com

About the Author

Richard LeBrun CFB, CCIM

Having had the opportunity to own and operate several businesses throughout his thirty-year career, Rich LeBrun is passionate about coaching small business owners enabling them to increase their profit margins, successfully introduce new product lines and develop award-winning teams.

Whether you are an executive out of work, a woman re-entering the workforce, a veteran returning home from service or someone just not ready to retire, Rich wants to help those in life's transition navigate through the exciting journey of selecting their franchise opportunity. Choosing the right franchise to own can be one of the most crucial and rewarding decisions one will make in a lifetime.

Rich is ready to successfully guide you through this process to find freedom and true passion in owning your own business.

Prior to becoming a franchise consultant, Rich was a Vice President with the largest commercial real estate company in Chicago and worked with pension funds and private equity groups.

Rich is a Certified Franchise Broker (CFB) and Certified Commercial Investment Manager (CCIM).

Made in the
USA
Lexington, KY